SECOND MANASSAS

SECOND MANASSAS

Longstreet's Attack and the Struggle for Chinn Ridge

SCOTT C. PATCHAN

POTOMAC BOOKS
WASHINGTON, D.C.

Library of Congress Cataloging-in-Publication Data
Patchan, Scott C., 1966–
  Second Manassas : Longstreet's attack and the struggle for Chinn Ridge /
Scott C. Patchan.—1st ed.
      p. cm.
  Includes bibliographical references and index.
  ISBN 978-1-59797-687-9 (hardcover : alk. paper)
  1. Bull Run, 2nd Battle of, Va., 1862. 2. Longstreet, James, 1821–1904.
I. Title.
  E473.77.P37 2011
  973.7'32–dc22

                                                        2011013354

Printed in the United States of America on acid-free paper that meets the
American National Standards Institute Z39-48 Standard.

Potomac Books
22841 Quicksilver Drive
Dulles, Virginia 20166

First Edition

10 9 8 7 6 5 4 3 2 1

Contents

Maps

Foreword

HISTORIANS LOVE TO HAVE the last word. Indeed, most who write a book fantasize (comically, in retrospect) that no one will ever need lay pen to paper (or fingers to keyboard, in this newfangled age) once their tome is safely tucked away on the shelves of a bookstore. In 1991 when I hit the "save" key for the last time on my book about the Second Battle of Manassas, I exalted briefly that no one would ever have to even think about the battle again. They just need to sit back and consume word and wisdom. How wrong I was.

Egotistical exaltation quickly gave way to the reality of errors, misjudgments, and incompleteness. Soon after the book's publication, I readily adopted the more socially palatable—and realistic—position that my work was very much a first step for modern researchers. It became my hope that, rather than being the "last word" on the battle, the book would stimulate more interest, argument, and investigation. Elaboration and correction, I timidly concluded, were good things—and inevitable, too.

With Scott Patchan's intensive look at the fight for Chinn Ridge, elaboration and correction have come in magnificent form.

No portion of the Second Manassas campaign deserves a closer examination than the fighting on Chinn Ridge. On Benjamin Chinn's farm occurred some of the most intense sustained combat of the war—fighting that sucked a stream of Union and Confederate regiments in and expelled them as bloody remnants. What happened that Saturday afternoon resolved the entire Second Manassas campaign, determining the magnitude of Confederate victory (or Union disaster, for those so inclined). Few pieces of landscape hallowed during the war can claim such an obvious, decisive connection to the outcome of a major battle.

Beyond the site's significance, the complexity of the fighting also demands a closer look than has been given until now. When I wrote about Second Manassas, I spread out my notes, tried to fit the Chinn Ridge pieces together, and offered the best version I could of a very muddled event. From the first, I knew I had written an oversimplification. I knew that I had sometimes sought refuge in vague generalities—using broad brush strokes when fine detail was warranted. And on still other occasions, I flat took guesses based on the sources available. (I may be breaking some unspoken code by admitting as much, but anyone who has written about a major battle knows that an author's confident verbiage often cloaks virtual befuddlement.)

Scott Patchan has stepped into this historical morass armed with new sources, a detailed knowledge of the ground (absolutely indispensable when writing of a battle), and a fresh perspective. He has forged a monograph that clears much of the mud, sharpens the detail, and removes much of the guesswork involved in previous works dealing with the climactic clash at Second Manassas. For me, this is a humbling work—demonstrating just how incomplete my own efforts on the subject have been. For the historical community, this book does more than just provide new detail; it provides new understanding of events and characters—a marked contrast to so many works on so many other battles (does Gettysburg come to mind?).

Patchan's book is also a vivid human story. Here are new perspectives on the great and small personalities of the day: James Longstreet, Nathaniel McLean, John Hood, Montgomery Corse, Zealous Tower, Irvin McDowell, and many others. Moreover, he takes this epoch of battle and views it incessantly through personal eyes, weaving accounts rarely used, previously misused, or not used at all. Even if you are not interested in Chinn Ridge or Second Manassas, you should still read this book, because it is foremost about people and their reaction to the greatest of all human fears and challenges.

Scott Patchan has done history and students of the Civil War a great service. It is hard to imagine someone outdoing this work. Scott, when you receive your first copies of this book in the mail, you may indeed do some gloating; your readers can sit back and consume word and wisdom about Chinn Ridge. This book will surely be the last word.

At least for a very long time.

John J. Hennessy
Fredericksburg, VA

Acknowledgments

ANY AUTHOR KNOWS THERE ARE myriad individuals who contribute their time and knowledge to help him or her successfully complete a project. Anyone researching and writing on the Second Manassas Campaign must be greatly indebted to John Hennessy. Only his generosity and dedication to Civil War history surpass his knowledge on that campaign. *Return to Bull Run* and *Second Manassas Battlefield Map Study* are definitive accounts of this campaign. All subsequent works on the Second Battle of Manassas must build on the solid foundation of source material and analysis he has compiled and generously shares with other students of the campaign.

Marine Corps historian J. Michael Miller provided generous assistance by reading the manuscript and suggesting more emphasis on the "big picture." National Park Service historians Ray Brown, Jim Burgess, Ed Rauss, and Mac Wyckoff kindly reviewed drafts and suggested improvements. Their efforts have resulted in the making of a more readable book. Thanks are also in order for the staff members of the Manassas National Battlefield visitor center who permitted me to use the extensive library and manuscript collection on Second Manassas on scores of occasions.

I am also greatly indebted to Col. John C. McAnaw, USA (Ret.), of Fairfax, Virginia. John has served as a sounding board for interpretations and was always ready to review them from a pure military perspective. For several years, John has provided me with input on a wide variety of Civil War topics and taught me to be more skeptical in my analysis of sources. Most important, he sketched the detailed maps contained in this book, without which it would be incomplete.

Many thanks are in order for Gary Ecelbarger, who took the time to read the manuscript (some of it more than once) and suggest improvements. This book is a better work thanks to his efforts. I would like to thank Steve Burr of Tallmadge, Ohio, for providing excellent sources on the 55th Ohio at Second Manassas. Larry Strayer of Dayton, Ohio, was generous as usual in supplying photographs and general assistance on Ohio references. Brock Nicely of Staunton, Virginia, graciously shared his thoughts on, and material from, the Palmetto Sharpshooters with me, shedding new light on the role of Micah Jenkins's brigade at Second Manassas. Thanks are in order to Lt. Col. Henry W. Persons Jr. of Maryland for his assistance in providing information on George T. "Tige" Anderson's Georgians. My appreciation is due to James J. Baldwin III of South Carolina for sending me information on the 5th South Carolina Infantry. Dave Purschwitz of the Manassas Museum shared his files on the 8th Virginia Infantry with me. In addition to those named, many others contributed to the success of this project.

I also want to thank all of my editors at Potomac, Elizabeth Demers, acquisitions; Don McKeon, reviewer; Julie Gutin, production editor; and Kathryn Owens, copyeditor. Their efforts greatly improved this work and helped me to develop as a writer.

Special recognition is owed to my son, Andrew, who has spent uncountable hours of his youth roaming around Manassas National Battlefield with me in order to follow the action of Longstreet's attack. Andrew's contributions include refighting the action around Young's Branch with snowballs during the heavy snowfalls that hit northern Virginia in 1995. My daughter Elena accompanied me on many visits to the park, although being a toddler at the time she preferred throwing rocks into Young's Branch and playing in the water to hiking the battlefield. Our youngest child, Sophia, also joined me on some walks through the Stuart's Hill portion of the park, although she ended up being carried most of the time. Thanks also to my wife, Nancy, who made the time available for me to work on this book and reviewed the manuscript to make it a much more readable product.

Introduction

I FIRST VISITED MANASSAS National Battlefield in 1988. Like that of most visitors, my tour consisted of the standard visitor center overview and the First Bull Run loop trail on Henry Hill. It was not long, however, before I made subsequent visits and discovered the serene beauty and historical aura offered by Chinn Ridge. Its tranquillity allows visitors to visualize the battle raging across the dips and folds of the landscape without distraction from the busy roads that clog Manassas Battlefield.

Chinn Ridge further piqued my interest when I learned of the slashing Confederate attacks and the Union's heroic delaying action that occurred there during the Second Battle of Manassas. To my disappointment, I also learned that at that time no first-class history existed on Second Manassas. Left with few alternatives, I delved into *War of the Rebellion: Official Records of the Union and Confederate Armies*, which includes the officers' after-action reports, published memoirs, and regimental histories. I rapidly became acquainted with the personalities and valor of the men who fought on Chinn Ridge: Nathaniel McLean, John B. Hood, Zealous Tower, Montgomery Corse, and Henry Benning, to name only a few. The firsthand accounts of the officers and enlisted men told of the tremendous misery and suffering that occurred on Chinn Ridge on August 30, 1862.

In 1993 John Hennessy's highly acclaimed *Return to Bull Run: The Campaign and Battle of Second Manassas* was published, deepening my interest in Chinn Ridge. His work filled a void in Civil War literature and became a model for modern campaign and battle studies. Of the daunting task facing the Union troops on Chinn Ridge, Hennessy wrote, "If Hood, Evans and whatever other Confederates might arrive ousted them swiftly from Chinn Ridge, the way to Henry Hill would be open, and the Union army might be wrecked."[1]

Moreover, *Return to Bull Run* highlighted for me the importance of the fighting on Chinn Ridge within the context of the military situation in Virginia at that time. The Second Battle of Manassas, Hennessy argued, "brought Lee and the Confederacy to the edge of their greatest opportunity. No victory of the war so thoroughly cleared the strategic table for the Confederates. The route north lay unencumbered. A victory on Union soil held the potential to force a swift and happy political solution to the war."[2]

According to Hennessy, the Confederate counterattack on August 30, 1862, "would come as close to destroying a Union army as any ever would." If it had not been for the Herculean efforts of the Union troops on Chinn Ridge, Lee very well might have severely crippled Maj. Gen. John Pope's Army of Virginia and the three attached corps serving with it from the Army of the Potomac. Such an occurrence may have proven disastrous to the Union cause in 1862, for the circumstances that would have allowed for the Union army to be destroyed existed at Manassas on that hot August day in 1862.[3]

This opportunity largely presented itself from John Pope's refusal to act on the military reality of the situation at Manassas for most of that day. Pope had massed virtually his entire army north of the Warrenton Turnpike in front of Maj. Gen. Thomas J. "Stonewall" Jackson. The Union commander ignored the presence of Maj. Gen. James Longstreet's wing of Lee's army posted south of the turnpike. Despite repeated warnings of Longstreet's arrival on the battlefield on August 29, Pope simply refused to accept that reality until it was too late. If Longstreet could rapidly slice through the token Union forces in his front, the path to cut the Army of Virginia off from its line of retreat across Bull Run at the Stone Bridge would be cleared.

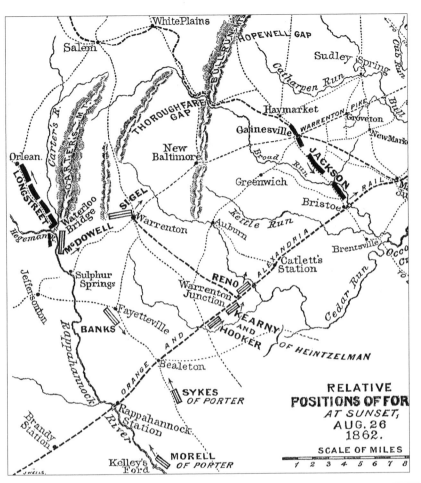

From Battles and Leaders of the Civil War *by Clarence Clough Buel and Robert Underwood Johnston (New York: The Century Co., 1884–1887).*

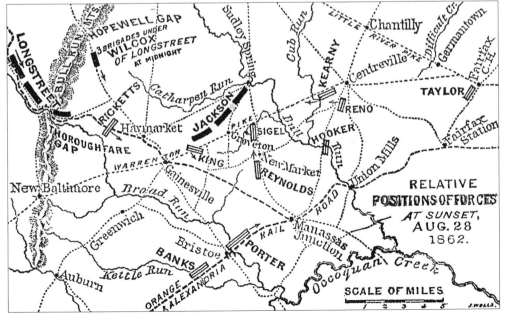

By massing his troops in front of Jackson, Pope had forfeited his advantage in manpower. The dense number of troops could have fallen easy prey to the Confederate forces operating around it. Only the Federals on the edges could return fire at the attacking Southerners. The troops in the inside ranks would have to endure casualties without being able to shoot back—a most demoralizing proposition for combat soldiers.

In addition to Pope's deluded view of the military situation on the battlefield, the area's topography would have aided Lee's destructive blow against the Army of Virginia. The rugged and precipitous slopes of Bull Run's banks limited the army's ability to retreat without the bridge. Further, the stream looped north of Bull Run Bridge to the west. This feature combined with the position of Jackson's wing would have served as a corral, funneling Pope's retreating army into a relatively small area. The quality of the few available fords there would have ensured confusion, possibly a panic that exceeded anything at First Bull Run in 1861. Much, if not all, of Pope's artillery would not have been able to negotiate the steep banks and rugged crossings. As Jackson and Longstreet pressed in from the west, north, and south, chunks of the Federal army could have been cut off and captured.

In all likelihood, Pope would have lost control of thousands of soldiers as they fled toward Washington with Maj. Gen. James E. B. "Jeb" Stuart's cavalry stalking them along the way. It would have taken weeks to reorganize and reequip the rabble that managed to escape into an effective army. Maj. Gen. George B. McClellan would have been forced to use his two intact corps from the Army of the Potomac and the small, battered corps of Maj. Gen. Nathaniel P. Banks, which had not participated in Second Manassas, as the nucleus of a force to defend Washington.

As for the impact of such a defeat of Pope's army, the Second Battle of Winchester provides a fitting example for its effects. At Second Winchester, Confederate major general Richard S. Ewell had cut off then Union major general Robert H. Milroy's smaller army from its escape routes to the north. In the end, Ewell placed almost 50 percent of Milroy's army out of action as official casualties. Thousands of survivors escaped singly and in small detachments, but may as well have been captured, for they were of no use from a military perspective. For weeks, they turned up at remote locations in Maryland, Pennsylvania, and West Virginia. It then took several months to fully assemble and reorganize these units. From a morale standpoint, some units never recovered from the psychological damage of such a devastating defeat, and never regained their combat efficiency and confidence.

In a larger sense, a defeat inflicted on Pope's Army of Virginia may have proven fatal to the Union in 1862. But the stout resistance of the Union troops on Chinn Ridge that afternoon slowed Lee's advance and stirred the fog of war to such a degree that the Union's nightmare scenario did not become a reality. Although driven from the ridge, the Union troops prevailed in the battle for a time—time that allowed Pope to shift elements of his massed army to Henry Hill in order to cover a relatively organized retreat toward Washington.

One

"TAKE CARE OF YOURSELF"

*As the sun sank behind the Bull Run Mountains on August 30, 1862,
casting shadows across the Virginia Piedmont, Col. Nathaniel McLean rode
alongside the shattered remnant of his Ohio brigade. A few hours earlier,
the brigade had numbered fifteen hundred Buckeye soldiers, but their heroic
stand atop Chinn Ridge had sadly reduced that number. A blue-eyed, bushy-
bearded warrior from Cincinnati, McLean approached Col. John C. Lee,
commander of the 55th Ohio Volunteer Infantry. The two men exchanged
somber glances and shook hands without speaking. They didn't have to. The
tears streaming down their cheeks plainly told of the suffering their soldiers
had endured during the Second Battle of Bull Run.[1]*

THE GENESIS OF THE SECOND MANASSAS Campaign came about on June 26,
1862, when President Abraham Lincoln appointed Maj. Gen. John Pope
commander of the Union's newest force, the Army of Virginia. It consisted
of three corps that had previously operated independently of one another
in northern Virginia and the Shenandoah Valley. These troops had participated to one degree or another in tracking down Stonewall Jackson in the
Shenandoah Valley Campaign in the spring of 1862. That campaign ended
terribly for the Union cause and played an important role in saving Richmond from capture by Maj. Gen. George B. McClellan's Army of the Potomac.
When Lincoln appointed Pope to command the second major Union force

in Virginia, the president had expected him to rejuvenate the soldiers of the Army of Virginia into a force that could contend with the proud veterans of Gen. Robert E. Lee's Army of Northern Virginia. Even as Lincoln assigned Pope to command, Lee's army was in the very process of defeating McClellan in front of Richmond, which added to the administration's expectations for John Pope.

General Lee's victory at Richmond in the Seven Days Battles established him and his army as a force that was capable of defeating McClellan's larger Army of the Potomac. While Lee did not always prevail at the tactical level and endured defeats such as Malvern Hill, he kept McClellan off balance by doing the unexpected and launching an audacious series of sledgehammer attacks that stole the initiative from him. In a matter of one week, Lee had forced McClellan from the gates of Richmond to Harrison's Landing, nearly twenty miles down the James River. Although the Lincoln administration hoped that McClellan could retrieve the situation, he remained ensconced at the landing, convinced that Lee greatly outnumbered the Potomac army. Instead of taking action against the enemy, "Little Mac" characteristically insisted that Lincoln reinforce him with "rather much over than much under 100,000 men." He believed that Lee had at least 200,000 men at Richmond. In reality, Lee did not even have 90,000 men in his army, but with McClellan's mind-set, Lee had little fear of a renewed offensive against Richmond from the Army of the Potomac.[2]

While Pope was acquainting himself with his army, two major generals, Thomas J. "Stonewall" Jackson and James Longstreet, had emerged as the premier division commanders in Lee's Army of Northern Virginia. Jackson did so based largely on the successes he had achieved in the Shenandoah Valley. He had put in a rather uncharacteristically dull performance during the Seven Days Battles. Nevertheless, Lee had come to count on Jackson, and Longstreet especially, during the campaign against McClellan. When Lee reorganized the Army of Northern Virginia into two wings upon the termination of the Seven Days Battles, he assigned Longstreet command of the right wing and Jackson command of the left. American military history had seldom witnessed such a talented combination of skill and ability fighting side by side in the same army.

In northern Virginia John Pope's appointment to command also signaled a change in the way the Union would conduct the war with President Lincoln's blessing. Up until the time Pope assumed command of the Army of Virginia, the Union armies had gone out of their way to respect the Southern property rights, including the return of runaway slaves. In the Army of the Potomac, McClellan had issued strict orders against plundering and foraging among the South's civilian populace. Breakdowns in discipline no doubt occurred, but such actions were never sanctioned by the Army of the Potomac's high command. In contrast, Pope ordered the Army of Virginia to "subsist upon the country," taking crops and livestock from Southern civilians to provide for his army's needs. He implemented a system of harsh retaliation whenever guerrillas attacked his troops by burning the home they had been using. Further, the home's occupants would be arrested and imprisoned. He also instituted a policy of arresting "all disloyal male citizens" who came within the reach of Pope's army. These measures were popular with the rank and file. One enlisted man wrote in a letter, "They are objectionable only in so far as they are not literally and completely enforced."[3]

John Pope had much more on his agenda than carrying out this harsher mode of warfare. His force was an army in name only, and to him belonged the task of forging it into an efficient implement of war. Pope's Army of Virginia consisted of three corps, each commanded by men of questionable military reputation. Maj. Gen. Franz Sigel, a German expatriate, commanded the I Corps. Although he had rallied many Missouri Germans to the Union cause, he proved ineffective as a combat leader at the Battle of Wilson's Creek in 1861. His corps consisted of three divisions, with many of the troops being German or of German descent, held in low esteem by many native-born American troops. Maj. Gen. Nathaniel P. Banks led the II Corps that guarded the Orange and Alexandria Railroad during the Second Battle of Manassas. Banks had shown his inability during the 1862 Valley Campaign, when Jackson pummeled him at the battles of Front Royal and Winchester. Maj. Gen. Irvin McDowell, the failed Union commander from the First Battle of Bull Run, or Manassas (July 21, 1861), held the reins of command for the III Corps. The small IX Corps, led by Maj. Gen. Jesse L.

Reno, joined Pope in early August after operating on the Carolina coast. Later that month, Maj. Gen. Samuel P. Heintzelman's III Corps and Maj. Gen. Fitz John Porter's V Corps (both from McClellan's Potomac army) were attached to the Army of Virginia. In all, Pope had at least 70,000 men to confront Lee's 55,000-man Army of Northern Virginia.

Pope's method of warfare created uproar throughout the South. The *Richmond Dispatch* declared Pope an "enemy of humanity"; Lee deemed him "a miscreant." When Lee learned that Pope had occupied Culpeper in central Virginia on July 12, he ordered Jackson to nearby Gordonsville with two divisions from Richmond. At Gordonsville, Jackson would not only keep a wary eye on Pope but also protect the vital Virginia Central Railroad line that connected Richmond with the Piedmont and the Shenandoah Valley, the breadbasket of Lee's army. Jackson arrived at Gordonsville with his vanguard on July 19, where he monitored Pope's activities from a distance. Lee hoped to transfer the active theater of operations from Richmond to central Virginia in order to drive out Pope's army. To that end, Lee reinforced Jackson with Maj. Gen. A. P. Hill's large division and an additional brigade. With these reinforcements also came heightened expectations of Jackson's command, and in this case Lee told Stonewall, "I want Pope to be suppressed."[4]

Lee couldn't have asked for a better man than Jackson for the assignment. He wasted no time and began the campaign against Pope in earnest by attacking Banks's isolated corps of Pope's army at Cedar Mountain near Culpeper on August 9. Banks's force gained the upper hand in combat early on, but Jackson's numbers ultimately drove the Federals from the battlefield, adding more laurels to his reputation. Despite Banks's defeat, Pope did not shy away from confrontation but rushed McDowell's corps to Culpeper, which nullified Jackson's manpower advantage over Banks. Although Stonewall prudently withdrew his army to the south bank of the Rapidan River, his victory at Cedar Mountain had upset John Pope's timetable and was the first in a series of events that caused the Union general to lose focus.[5]

Four days after that battle, Lee upped the ante. He ordered Longstreet to Gordonsville with ten brigades via the Virginia Central Railroad while Stuart rode there with his cavalry. Finally, on August 15, Lee personally went to Gordonsville on the Virginia Central Railroad and assumed command of the Army of Northern Virginia to implement his campaign to "suppress" that "miscreant" from Illinois, John Pope.[6]

Lee initially hoped to strike Pope's army while it was in a precarious position along the Rapidan River. There, Pope's army rested within a triangular peninsula formed by the confluence of the Rapidan and Rappahannock rivers, and Lee intended to drive his army into the junction of those streams. However, Pope readily recognized the danger posed to the Army of Virginia and deftly withdrew to the north bank of the Rappahannock, the new line of demarcation between the opposing armies.[7]

With a vastly strengthened Confederate force in his front, Pope now planned to remain on the defensive and wait until reinforcements from McClellan's Army of the Potomac arrived. Only after he was confident in his army's strength would Pope consider offensive operations. The delayed arrival of these troops ultimately hindered his options in central Virginia. McClellan moved at his customarily snail-like pace in transferring troops from the peninsula to Fredericksburg, despite receiving orders to that effect from the Lincoln administration on August 4. By August 18 not a single soldier of McClellan's army had boarded the transports. They finally began to arrive at Fredericksburg on August 22, eighteen days after the original orders had been issued.[8]

However, before Pope could assemble his army and develop an operational plan, Robert E. Lee moved first. On August 25 he unleashed Stonewall Jackson with 25,000 men on a sweeping flank march around Pope's right flank, quietly leaving Longstreet to confront Pope along the Rappahannock River. Jackson slipped around Pope's right flank undetected and marched straight into the rear of Pope's army, still situated along the Rappahannock. To make the fast-paced march a success, the Confederate infantry traveled light and often ran short of rations, but their sacrifices paid off. On August 26 Jackson captured Pope's supply depot at Manassas Junction. "What a time it was," recalled a soldier of the Stonewall brigade's 2nd Virginia Infantry, "half starved and worn out, we suddenly found ourselves turned loose among car loads of everything good to eat and drink and smoke." Eat, drink, and smoke they did, so much so that Jackson had to send a provost guard to the junction to destroy the alcohol the troops had discovered.[9]

While Jackson's men feasted at Manassas Junction on August 27, Federal forces began closing in on him. There was always the threat that Pope would strike northward, and that Jackson might find himself between Pope and Union forces marching out of Washington. In fact, a regiment that had marched out from Washington's defense attacked Jackson's troops at the junction that very morning but was quickly driven back. No sooner had that threat dissipated than two trainloads of Union troops arrived at the Bull Run Bridge on the Orange and Alexandria Railroad. Again, Jackson lashed out and attacked the probing Federals, ultimately repelling their advance. From Pope's army to the south, Maj. Gen. Joseph Hooker's division from Heintzelman's III Corps attacked Jackson's rear guard at Bristoe Station later the same day.

When Pope learned that Jackson had gotten in his rear at Manassas Junction, the Federal commander declared, "We shall bag the whole crowd!" As expected by almost everyone but Pope, Jackson failed to cooperate. He quickly and quietly departed the junction on the night of August 27 and marched his troops to the scene of the First Battle of Manassas, where he concealed them in a large wooded tract situated behind an unfinished railroad bed.[10]

The following day Pope's army searched for Jackson's force without success. Late that balmy summer afternoon of August 28, Jackson revealed his position as McDowell's III Corps marched past along the Warrenton Turnpike on its way from Gainesville to Centreville. When the Union troops appeared, Jackson roused his men and launched a disjointed offensive against a brigade of hearty Westerners from Indiana and Wisconsin. In the ensuing engagement, the Union and Confederate soldiers fought each other to a standstill at Brawner's Farm. However, Brawner's Farm was not the only engagement that occurred on August 28. Earlier that afternoon, Longstreet's wing had brushed aside Brig. Gen. James B. Ricketts's division of McDowell's corps at the Battle of Thoroughfare Gap. Ricketts's division had belatedly tried to block Longstreet's advance through Thoroughfare Gap in the Bull Run Mountains, only eight miles west of Brawner's Farm. That Longstreet had approached so near to Pope seemed to be of little consequence to the Union commander at the time.

Instead, the engagement at Brawner's Farm convinced Pope that he had finally isolated the mighty Jackson. To Pope, it only remained for him to crush Stonewall. To this end, Pope ordered his corps' commanders to concentrate along the Warrenton Turnpike in Jackson's front and attack him early the next morning, August 29. A lack of cooperation among Pope's subordinates started the day off wrong, and the attack, instead of being a massive coordinated effort, turned into a series of disjointed assaults against Jackson's strong line behind the unfinished railroad bed. Time and time again, an unsupported Union force pierced the Confederate line only to be thrown back by a well-timed Southern counterattack.

But the most important event of August 29 at Manassas occurred outside the arena of combat. Longstreet's wing of Lee's army joined Jackson on the battlefield near Brawner's Farm after marching a leisurely eight miles from Thoroughfare Gap led by Lee himself. The news of Longstreet's arrival rejuvenated the spirits of Jackson's fatigued men. Whereas they had heretofore understood that Pope greatly outnumbered Jackson, after Longstreet's arrival they eagerly awaited Pope's next move and only feared that he might withdraw before the Confederate army could inflict more damage on the Federal Army of Virginia. Despite the failure of every assault that Pope launched on August 29, he deluded himself into believing that Jackson had experienced the worst of the day's fighting. What's more, Pope remained so focused on Jackson that the Union commander foolishly ignored repeated warnings of Longstreet's arrival. While there was strong evidence telling of Longstreet's reinforcements, Pope remained convinced that the Confederates were preparing to retreat. Even after one of Pope's divisions engaged one of Longstreet's divisions in a twilight affair on August 29, the Federal commander still disregarded Longstreet's presence on the battlefield. Instead, Pope planned to pursue the "beaten" Jackson on August 30.[11]

BUCK HILL

Early on the morning of August 30, Brig. Gen. Marsena R. Patrick, a brigade commander in Maj. Gen. Irvin McDowell's corps of Pope's army, spied one of Longstreet's divisions moving west on the Warrenton Turnpike toward the Bull Run Mountains. Patrick concluded that the Confederates were withdrawing and passed this inaccurate information on to McDowell, who in turn referred it to Pope. The Federal commander had eagerly hoped for just this sort of intelligence. In actuality, the Confederate division had overshot the main Confederate line when it deployed the previous night. It was only falling back to conform to the general Confederate line and to avoid unnecessary exposure to the accurate fire of the Union artillery posted in force on Dogan Ridge. Nevertheless, Pope wired the U.S. War Department that "the enemy is retreating toward the mountains," with no corroborating evidence.[12]

At seven o'clock that morning, Pope gathered his senior generals for a council of war at Pope's headquarters on Buck Hill near the intersection of the Warrenton Turnpike and Sudley Road. General Heintzelman, commanding the III Corps of the Army of the Potomac, recorded the proceedings:

> There was great doubt about the position of the enemy. It was decided at a council composed of McDowell, Sigel, Porter, Pope and me to attack his [Jackson's] left flank with three Corps—McDowell's, Porter's and mine. McDowell and I went and reconnoitered and were of the impression that the enemy was not in force on their left. We met Sigel as we returned and he holds the center and he was of the impression they had left. When we got to Pope, he had seen one of our wounded and he reported the enemy had been moving off towards our left and Thoroughfare Gap all night. It was now concluded that he had left and we should pursue.[13]

Thus, Pope would formulate his plans based on a completely false assessment of Lee's dispositions and intentions.

Maj. Gen. Fitz John Porter arrived near the conclusion of the council with a dire warning for the Union commander. His V Corps, Army of the Potomac, had spent most of the preceding day on the far left of the Union line. When he attempted to advance, he ran into Longstreet's deploying troops. Porter fervently attempted to convince Pope that the Confederate line extended well beyond the Union left flank. Pope would not listen to any evidence that contradicted his plans, especially when the man bearing the message was a close confidant of McClellan's; the latter's chances of regaining command of the Union army in Virginia hinged on Pope's failure. Brig. Gen. John F. Reynolds, whose division of Pennsylvania Reserves occupied a position in Longstreet's front, lent Porter verbal support, but Pope still refused to believe these competent Union officers. He also received several warnings from his right wing, which indicated that Jackson still occupied the railroad cut and had not retired as Patrick's report indicated. Instead, Pope selectively relied on only sketchy information that foretold of the Confederate withdrawal, which he so badly wished for. Instead of acting on the overwhelming evidence that clearly indicated Longstreet's presence, Pope readied his army to pursue Jackson's supposedly beaten and retreating Confederates. To this end, Pope shifted the vast majority of his army to the northern side of the Warrenton Turnpike to attack Jackson.

Still hoping to change Pope's mind before disaster struck, Reynolds returned to his command south of the Warrenton Turnpike and launched a reconnaissance mission shortly after noon. Reynolds found enemy skirmishers posted at right angles to his battle line, with Confederate cavalry behind them masking Longstreet's troops. These skirmishers aimed and shot at Reynolds, who ran a "gauntlet of a heavy fire" until reaching the rear of his division. Then he galloped back to Pope's headquarters on Buck Hill where he arrived a little after one o'clock. Reynolds rode up to Pope and gasped, "The enemy is turning our left." A dismissive and unconcerned Pope replied, "Oh, I guess not." Nevertheless, Pope sent Brig. Gen. John Buford, a trusted cavalry commander, to investigate the accuracy of Reynolds's report with his cavalry. He made no alteration, however, to his planned pursuit of Jackson. Exactly what, if anything, Buford reported back to Pope is uncertain. The cavalryman maneuvered his brigade on the army's left, where he later stymied an effort by the Confederate cavalry to cross Bull Run and interdict Pope's line of retreat.[14]

Although Pope gave Reynolds's report little regard, McDowell returned to the front with the Pennsylvania Reserves and examined the situation.

After scanning the Confederate position, McDowell ordered Reynolds to withdraw his reserves to Chinn Ridge located in the southwestern quadrant formed by the intersection of the Warrenton Turnpike and Sudley Road. On Dogan Ridge north of the Warrenton Turnpike, General Sigel received "repeated reports that the enemy was shifting his troops from the Gainesville Turnpike to [Lee's] right." Sigel dispatched the 4th New York Cavalry to patrol the army's left flank and "to scout the country as far as they could go." Sigel also sent the 55th Ohio to Chinn Ridge to establish communication with Reynolds's Pennsylvania Reserves. One hour later, a messenger from the 4th New York informed Sigel that the cavalry had located the enemy and "the latter were moving against our left." Sigel hurried the messenger to Pope's headquarters with this "fresh" information.[15]

As had become the norm, Sigel's information had little impact on Pope. Despite the now-overwhelming flow of intelligence on the full extent of the Confederate dispositions, Pope remained aloof to the danger that Lee's army posed to the Army of Virginia. With an apathetic wave, Pope motioned toward Henry Hill and Chinn Ridge and told his chief of staff, Col. George Ruggles, to have Sigel send a brigade over to "that bald hill." Even though Pope actually wanted the brigade placed on the western slope of Henry Hill, Ruggles thought that his commander meant Chinn Ridge, so careless and general was Pope's sweeping wave. Given the strength of Longstreet's force, Pope's response represented a mere token gesture that was likely designed to placate those officers who fretted about the safety of the Federal left flank; it certainly did not represent any real indication of concern on the part of the Federal commander. Pope's decisions had put his army at risk, and its fate now rested in the calloused hands of its soldiers and front-line commanders. Although Pope did not recognize, or more likely refused to accept, the consequences of ignoring Longstreet, every private in the Union army worried "lest the Johnnies should reach the Warrenton pike and cause irreparable injury to the Union army."[16]

DOGAN RIDGE

Around two o'clock that afternoon, Ruggles rode from Buck Hill to Sigel's headquarters on Dogan Ridge. He found the German conversing with

BATTLEFIELD OVERVIEW

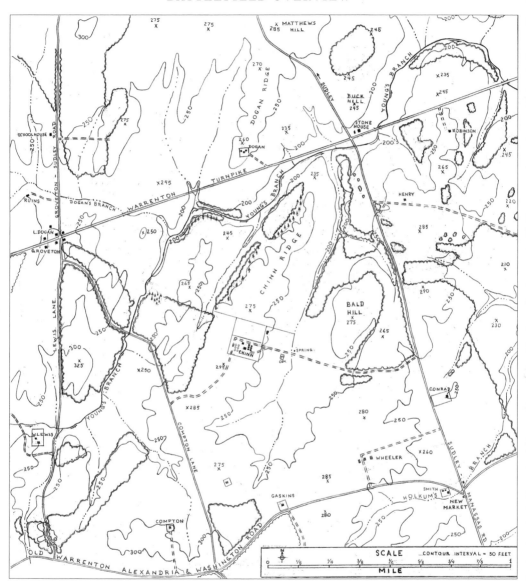

John C. McAnaw

a group of officers, including Brig. Gen. Robert Schenck, a division commander, and Col. Nathaniel C. McLean, an acting brigadier. Ruggles quickly interjected and instructed Sigel to place a brigade "upon the bald-headed hill" south of the Warrenton Turnpike.

"What bald hill?" retorted Sigel. McLean pointed to Chinn Ridge and asked Ruggles if that were the hill in question. Ruggles replied, "General Pope directed me to order the brigade to occupy that bald hill," as he imitated Pope's vague wave toward Henry Hill and Chinn Ridge. A staff officer, Capt. Edward H. Allen of the 73rd Ohio, witnessed the event and concluded, "Ruggles did not feel confident of his own knowledge of this specific position which this brigade was to occupy," and only offered a verbatim repetition of General Pope's order. With no further specification on the position forthcoming from Ruggles, Sigel ordered Schenck to send McLean's brigade and Capt. Michael Wiedrich's battery to support Reynolds's Pennsylvania Reserves posted on the southwest face of Chinn Ridge.[17]

CHINN RIDGE

Nathaniel McLean was born the son of Ohio congressman John McLean and his wife on February 2, 1815. McLean spent his childhood and adolescent years in Ridgeville, Ohio, northeast of Cincinnati. He later attended college in Kentucky; and ultimately earned a law degree from Harvard in 1838. Upon graduation, he returned home and practiced law in Cincinnati, and married the daughter of a prominent judge. She bore him four children but died suddenly from illness, leaving them motherless. McLean raised his children alone before finally remarrying in 1858.

McLean's father had become an associate justice on the United States Supreme Court in 1829 and served for thirty-one years. He was also mentioned as a perennial presidential nominee but never received the nod. In his most notable act on the court, Justice McLean wrote the dissenting opinion for the controversial *Dred Scott v. Sandford* in 1857. This ruling opened the door for unrestricted slavery in the territories and declared that a slave remains a slave, even if residing in a free state. Justice McLean took umbrage at such a notion; in his dissent, he cited the "rule of freedom" and spoke out against slavery. As a result, abolitionists throughout the North adopted Justice McLean as their champion. And when war broke out, Nathaniel McLean joined the Union army, carrying his father's judicial fight onto the battlefield.[18]

McLean recruited and organized the 75th Ohio Infantry, becoming its first colonel in September 1861. His first serious action came on May 8, 1862, when he led the 25th and 75th Ohio Regiments at the Battle of McDowell in the Shenandoah Valley, charging up a steep mountainside against Stonewall Jackson's Southerners. Although attacking, McLean inflicted more than twice the casualties on the Confederates as his Ohioans suffered. McLean's commander, Brig. Gen. Robert H. Milroy, praised McLean and his men for their "undaunted bravery" in the face of a superior foe, and the "courage and zeal" with which the Ohioans maintained their position. At McDowell, McLean and his men "proved themselves to be true representatives of the American citizen-soldier" in Milroy's view.[19]

When McLean arrived at Chinn Ridge on August 30, he posted Wiedrich's four-gun battery on Reynolds's right flank. McLean positioned his three infantry regiments in column by division on the eastern slope of Chinn Ridge, a short distance behind the guns. McLean's fourth regiment, Col. John C. Lee's 55th Ohio, remained in position on the northern end of Chinn Ridge to partially cover the five hundred yards between Sigel's corps on the Warrenton Turnpike and Reynolds's division on the ridge. After deploying his command, McLean then reported to Reynolds, who still harbored concern for safety of the army's left flank. The relieved Pennsylvanian told McLean, "I will call upon you when necessary."[20]

While McLean posted his brigade on Chinn Ridge, Pope's "pursuit" of the supposedly withdrawing Confederate army had begun. In an effort that rivaled Pickett's Charge at Gettysburg, Pope hurled Porter's V Corps, reinforced by a division from McDowell, and some of Reno's troops at Jackson's position behind the unfinished railroad north of the Warrenton Turnpike. Although battered and fatigued from six days of marching and combat, Jackson's wing held firm and stopped Porter cold, aided by the artillery of Col. Stephen D. Lee. Porter's men retreated back up the turnpike toward Dogan

Ridge in considerable confusion, but Sigel's troops and the Union cavalry quickly restored order to Porter's retreat. Nevertheless, McDowell panicked when he saw Porter's men tumbling toward Dogan Ridge. He galloped over to Reynolds's position at the Chinn House. There McDowell, the failed Union commander from the First Battle of Manassas, excitedly gesticulated toward Porter's position, shouting, "General Reynolds! General Reynolds! Get every man into line and get away there." The removal of Reynolds's troops from Chinn Ridge proved to be the most fatal mistake of McDowell's ill-plagued military career. It was so stupendous that many Union soldiers went to their graves convinced that McDowell was a traitor and had intentionally removed Reynolds from Chinn Ridge so that Lee could obtain victory.[21]

Despite Reynolds's well-founded fears for the safety of the Union, he dutifully led the Pennsylvania Reserve division off Chinn Ridge to a position north of the Warrenton Turnpike. An astonished Nathaniel McLean first learned of Reynolds's departure when the Pennsylvanians marched across McLean's front toward the turnpike. McLean sent an officer to Reynolds, requesting orders for the Ohioans. Reynolds had none but warned the Ohioan of the strong Confederate force on the army's left flank and implored Colonel McLean "to take care of himself."[22]

Hearing this, McLean pondered his options but concluded that "the object was to maintain the position on Bald Hill [Chinn Ridge], and it seemed to me clearly my duty to hold the position until I was either ordered to retire or driven off by a superior force." In a futile attempt to cover the ground Reynolds had abandoned with three regiments, McLean's Ohioans marched to the crest of Chinn Ridge and deployed into line of battle. McLean shifted the 73rd and 25th Ohio Regiments to the left of Wiedrich's battery, where Reynolds's entire division had been in position and fronting westward. The 75th Ohio went into position on Wiedrich's right flank. McLean's fifteen hundred Ohioans now constituted the sole Union line of defense on Chinn Ridge. Without significant reinforcements, however, they stood virtually no chance of successfully defending it against Longstreet's thousands. Instead, the situation forced McLean to battle for time—the "most valuable element in all wars," according to Gen. William Tecumseh Sherman. McLean's decision to remain on Chinn Ridge proved pivotal and is all the more commendable given the atmosphere of distrust and intrigue that existed among the various factions of Pope's force.[23]

From the high ground on Dogan Ridge, Schenck and Sigel watched with concern as Reynolds's column abandoned Chinn Ridge and marched toward the Warrenton Turnpike, and speculated whose command it was. When the blue column reached the turnpike, Schenck exclaimed, "Those are Reynolds's troops. My brigade is unsupported. General Sigel, I must go there at once." Schenck jumped on his horse and galloped off to Chinn Ridge. Unfortunately, he did not take, or Sigel did not permit him to take, Brig. Gen. Julius S. Stahel's brigade of Schenck's own division with him to reinforce McLean's. It mattered little now as three Confederate divisions of Longstreet's wing had launched a massive counterattack on the south side of the Warrenton Turnpike. If the Southerners played their cards right, Pope's army might be destroyed largely because of Pope's virtual disregard for his left flank on the south side of the turnpike.[24]

Two

"Frenzied in Their Passions"

On the morning of August 30, General Lee assembled his all-star team of Longstreet, Jackson, and Stuart at his headquarters on Stuart's Hill to discuss the army's options and plans for the day. Lee hoped that Pope would continue his fruitless assaults, and so he deferred any offensive action and remained on the defensive. As the day progressed, Pope's inaction caught Lee off guard and left him wondering about the Union commander's intentions. Nevertheless, a confident Lee remained content to allow Pope the first move. If he didn't make it, Lee would send Jackson's wing on a flank march around Pope's right (northern) flank once again while Longstreet created a diversion in Pope's front. If all went well, as it had along the Rappahannock River, Jackson would once again interpose his force between Pope's army and Washington.[1]

Throughout the morning and early afternoon, Longstreet's twenty-eight thousand Confederates rested in the woods and fields upon a line stretching southward from Groveton on the Warrenton Turnpike to the Old Warrenton and Alexandria Road, a distance of nearly two miles. Shortly before three o'clock that afternoon, Longstreet issued orders for his divisions to be ready to launch a diversion in order to cover Jackson's proposed flank movement at five o'clock. Officers of the Texas Brigade in Brig. Gen. John B. Hood's division received instructions to remain "at attention and be ready to advance to attack the enemy whenever ordered." Longstreet instructed Brig. Gen. James L. Kemper to advance his division on Hood's right flank and conform to his movements. In the meantime, Kemper's three brigadiers rode forward and surveyed the terrain over which they were to advance.[2]

When Jackson repulsed Porter's attack shortly after three o'clock, Longstreet sensed an opportunity to capitalize on Pope's failed pursuit. Lee's War Horse, as Longstreet was sometimes called, instantly launched what would become one of the war's best-timed counterattacks. "At the critical moment I happened to be riding to the front of my line," wrote Longstreet, "I could plainly see the Federals as they rushed in heavy masses against the obstinate ranks on the Confederate left." While Longstreet watched the martial spectacle of Porter's attack, a courier from Jackson galloped up and requested assistance, which was almost instantly followed by another courier from Lee ordering him to do so. With little time to spare, Old Pete positioned the Dixie Artillery on a knoll east of Brawner's Woods where it fired into the flank of Porter's attacking column. Even more devastating to the Federal attack was the massed fire of Col. Stephen D. Lee's Artillery Battalion posted on Jackson's right flank. Aided by the Confederate cannoneers, Jackson repulsed Porter's attack.[3]

Upon this repulse, Longstreet ordered Hood to "push for the plateau at the Henry House in order to cut off the [Federal] retreat at the crossings of Young's Branch." If Hood attained that objective, then the continued existence of Pope's army as an effective fighting force might be in serious jeopardy. In John Bell Hood, Longstreet had perhaps the most aggressive general officer in the entire Confederacy setting the pace of the counterblow.

Standing six feet two, the blond Hood cut an impressive figure. He was born in Owingsville, Kentucky, as a doctor's son. Although his father encouraged him to take up medicine as a career, the younger Hood had idolized the military careers of his grandfathers, who had fought in the Revolutionary and Indian wars. The young man followed his heart and entered West Point, where he graduated forty-fourth out of fifty cadets in the class of 1853. After graduation he saw extensive service in Texas during his stint in the Regular

Army and experienced combat against Indians. When the Civil War erupted, Hood resigned from the U.S. Army and tendered his services to Kentucky. And when his native state did not secede, he traveled to Montgomery, Alabama, capital of the fledgling Confederacy, and received a lieutenant's commission in the Confederate Army.[4]

He was ordered to report to Robert E. Lee at Richmond, assigned the duty of organizing and training cavalry units, and rapidly promoted up the chain of command to the rank of major of the 3rd Virginia Cavalry. Hood saw minor action at Yorktown, where he impressed his superiors and was promoted to lieutenant colonel. His big break came in the fall of 1861, when the Confederate War Department was looking to replace Senator Lewis T. Wigfall as colonel of the 4th Texas Infantry. Because of his prewar military connection with Texas, Hood was given the job. By spring of 1862, he had been promoted to brigadier general of the Texas Brigade and led it with distinction throughout the Peninsula Campaign and Seven Days Battles.

During the Peninsula Campaign, Gen. Joseph E. Johnston had directed Hood "to feel the enemy gently and fall back." The pugnacious Kentuckian responded by routing a larger Federal force at Eltham's Landing on May 7, 1862, inflicting 194 Federal casualties while his brigade lost only 48 men. When the affair ended, Johnston asked Hood if he had just "given an illustration of the Texas idea of feeling an enemy gently and falling back." On June 27, 1862, at Gaines' Mill, Hood's brigade had shattered the Union lines, turning a stalemated battle into a decisive Confederate victory that set the tone for Lee's Seven Days campaign. Lee considered Hood's Texans a prime example of "daring and bravery" who could be depended on "in all tight places." "With a few more such regiments as those which General Hood now has," Lee told Wigfall, "I would feel much more confidence of the results of the campaign."[5] By Second Manassas, Hood was in command of a small division that was made up of his own Texas brigade, commanded by staff officer Capt. W. H. Sellers in Hood's name, and of Col. Evander M. Law's multistate brigade.[6]

Longstreet's attack order found Hood's men resting on the Cundiffe Farm just south of the Warrenton Turnpike across from Brawner's Farm. Colonel Law's brigade deployed on Hood's left north of the Warrenton

Turnpike, with the three brigades of Brig. Gen. Cadmus M. Wilcox farther to the north. Brig. Gen. Nathan G. Evans's South Carolinians waited for the attack to begin 250 yards behind the Texans. On Hood's right flank, Brig. Gen. James L. Kemper's division occupied the grounds of the William Lewis Farm. Longstreet directed Kemper to time his advance on Hood's movement.

South of Kemper, Brig. Gen. David R. "Neighbor" Jones's division anchored Longstreet's right flank near the Old Warrenton and Alexandria Road with instructions to advance on Kemper's right flank. Longstreet desired a coordinated attack in echelon by his entire wing. When Hood's division moved on the left, first Kemper and then Jones would continue the movement to the right, and sweep onto Henry Hill and cut the Union troops off from the bridge over Bull Run.[7]

The Texans realized that something was afoot by the sudden burst of activity. Couriers bearing dispatches to the various commands rode furiously back and forth. Orders directing the Texans to be ready to move soon came. They awaited the coming advance with "breathless anxiety." One Texan studied his comrades closely, noting,

> A close examination of the men would have satisfied anyone of the material of which they were composed. No vain boastings, no affected bravery in expectation of some distant battle, for the hour, the minute had come and the fiery ordeal was now to be tried. Coolly and calmly each man took his place in the ranks, pride lit up his countenance, and determination curled on every lip.[8]

Within a matter of minutes, Hood galloped up in front of the brigade and shouted, "Attention, Texas Brigade!" Cries of "Forward, March!" rang out along Hood's battle line. "Frenzied in their passions," Hood's men raised "the yell" and treaded toward Col. Gouverneur K. Warren's small Federal brigade a half mile distant. Similar scenes played out along Longstreet's battle line as his divisions readied for action and took up the advance.[9]

Warren's two regiments constituted the only Federal command in Hood's immediate front south of the Warrenton Turnpike. Warren, the

LONGSTREET'S ADVANCE

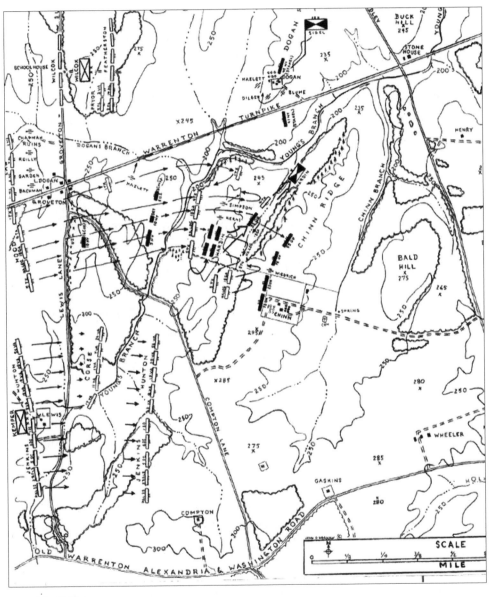

John C. McAnaw

visionary who later secured Little Round Top for the Union cause at Gettysburg, saw that Reynolds's withdrawal from Groveton prior to Porter's assault left a Federal battery "without support and our whole left flank was uncovered." Warren reported, "I immediately assumed the responsibility of occupying the place Reynolds's division had vacated, and made all the show of force I could." He posted six companies of the 10th New York (National Zouaves) in skirmish formation along a five-hundred-yard front across the edge of the woods lining the east side of Lewis Lane. The remaining four companies of National Zouaves waited in the woods behind the skirmishers as a reserve. Warren's other regiment, the 5th New York (Duryee's Zouaves), had deployed on a slight ridge, five hundred yards behind the National Zouaves. Lt. Charles "Cog" Hazlett's Battery D, 5th U.S. Artillery, occupied a hill overlooking Groveton about two hundred yards to the right front of the 5th New York.[10]

Warren's colorfully attired New Yorkers had gained a reputation for excellence in drill and performed capably during the Seven Days Battles for Richmond. Hood's Texans knew their reputation and were eager to confront them on the field of battle. Upon joining the Army of Virginia, these Zouaves had looked derisively on Pope's soldiers and freely expressed their disdain. Earlier in the battle, they had encountered some Wisconsin men from McDowell's corps who fought at Brawner's Farm and boasted, "We are going to teach you 'straw feet' how to fight." One of the rugged Western soldiers prophetically shot back, "Wait till you get where we have been. You'll get the slack taken out of your pantaloons and the swell out of your heads."[11]

Warren received a slight reinforcement from Lt. Andrew Sheridan's three-company detachment of the 3rd U.S. Infantry. Brig. Gen. George Sykes, commander of a division of Regular Army units, had deployed Sheridan's detachment south of the Warrenton Turnpike when Reynolds pulled back to Chinn Ridge earlier that afternoon. When Sykes's men fell back after Porter's repulse, Sheridan's contingent became separated from the Regular division. Sheridan saw Warren's brigade and fell in to fight with the Zouaves.[12]

In front of Warren's position, the approaching Texas Brigade guided its advance upon Col. Phillip A. Work's 1st Texas, whose left flank rested on the

Warrenton Turnpike. The 4th Texas advanced in line of battle on the right of the 1st Texas. The 18th Georgia, or "3rd Texas" as the Texas men respectfully dubbed it, occupied the brigade's center with the Hampton Legion on the Georgians' immediate right flank. Col. Jerome B. Robertson's 5th Texas anchored Hood's right flank.

Only 125 yards into the advance, confusion erupted on Hood's left flank. A staff officer informed Colonel Work that the 4th Texas had failed to advance on his right. Work halted the 1st Texas but soon realized that the 4th Texas was actually advancing 150 yards in front of the 1st Texas. For the Texans, this was only their first miscue of the day.

While the 1st Texas halted, the 5th Texas, Hampton Legion, and 18th Georgia advanced and encountered skirmishers from the 10th New York posted in the woods along Lewis Lane. The 4th Texas advanced as well but encountered no opposition in its front. Captain Sellers called out, "Forward skirmishers, and draw their fire before we get into the woods." The skirmishers obliged Sellers and seized a fence in front of the woods. The National Zouaves fired a single volley into the rapidly approaching Texans but failed to slow their progress. Hood's men fired back at the New Yorkers who "made for the rear at first class speed." Unable to rally on the reserves posted in the woods, the 10th New York retreated, with Hood's Carolinians, Georgians, and Texans in hot pursuit.[13]

Composed of the 5th New York and Sheridan's Regulars, Warren's battle line lay upon a cleared low ridge about 500 yards east of Lewis Lane. Dense woods surrounded the position on three sides, allowing the Confederates to approach within 150 yards in front before entering the open ground. Warren held this isolated position with no support on either flank. Before long, Pvt. Alfred Davenport of the 5th New York saw the National Zouaves "huddled in a heap and much scared," retreating toward Warren's line of battle. Following close behind the 10th New York, the Confederates reached the edge of the woods and spied the 5th New York waiting across the field. The Zouaves' conspicuous baggy red-and-blue uniforms prompted one hard-nosed Texan to write, "The sight of this regiment was both interesting and ridiculous in the extreme." The uniforms "served only to increase the merriment and enthusiasm" of Hood's troops.[14]

The 5th Texas worked its way through the woods, gaining the left flank and rear of Warren's position. Before the 5th New York even saw the approaching Confederates, Southern bullets pelted the Zouaves. Private Davenport reported, "Balls began to fly from the woods like hail." While the 5th Texas flanked the Zouaves, the Hampton Legion and 18th Georgia closed in from the front. Although the 5th New York attempted to resist the attack, the fugitives from the 10th New York blocked their field of fire. With unerring aim, Hood's brigade delivered incessant volleys of musketry, and Warren's troops fell in droves.[15]

When the National Zouaves finally cleared out, the 5th New York sent a weak volley into the approaching Confederates. Hood's men poured a devastating blast from their rifles into the Zouaves that literally tore them to pieces. Pvt. Andrew Coats of the 5th New York testified to the ferocity of the Confederate musketry when he grimly declared, "Not only were men wounded or killed, but they were riddled." The Texans rushed toward the Federals with a yell, firing as they advanced. One Texan described the 5th New York as "the worst whipped regiment that ever came to a field of battle." Those Federals who remained standing turned and ran. Most became casualties. Colonel Warren reported the loss of 102 Zouaves killed and 235 wounded, most of whom were left dead or dying where they fell. He also reported 75 missing.[16]

The survivors fled down the slope leading to Young's Branch, "a clear and pebbly bottomed branch." They splashed into the water and trudged up the ravine's eastern slope. The Texans chased after the fleeing Zouaves, yelling, "Stop, come back, you red breeched scoundrels." Hood's men followed the New Yorkers and fired continuously into their shattered masses. A few New Yorkers turned and fired a volley into the Confederates. A Texan wrote this praise: "Though few in number, they pluckily turned round and fired a volley into our midst and then disappeared." One New Yorker shot Lt. Col. John C. Upton of the 5th Texas in the forehead as he cheered his men across the run. Upton's lifeless body toppled into Young's Branch, but the 5th Texas pressed on. As the Southerners waded through the stream, they noticed that its waters ran bloodred from the scores of soldiers gunned down while crossing. Without pause, Hood's brigade started up the eastern slope of the ravine, where the 18th Georgia captured the 10th New York's battle flag.[17]

On Hood's left flank, the 1st Texas double-quicked to catch up to the 4th Texas and advanced against Cog Hazlett's battery. The Regulars repeatedly fired at the 1st Texas, slowing its advance, while the 4th Texas moved toward Young's Branch unopposed. Before the 1st Texas could charge the battery, the heroism of a Zouave from the 5th New York saved the guns from capture. Although he had already crossed to the east bank of Young's Branch, Pvt. James Webb saw Hazlett's gunners firing away at the 1st Texas and appearing to be unaware of Warren's disaster. Webb recrossed the stream and sprinted toward the battery under a hail of musket fire. Although painfully wounded, Webb reached the guns and warned Hazlett of his dilemma. Thanks to Webb, Hazlett safely withdrew all six pieces from their exposed position and redeployed in an orchard on Dogan Ridge. From his new position, Cog resumed hammering the 1st Texas, stalling its advance along the Warrenton Turnpike.[18]

Warren later gathered sixteen survivors from the 5th New York and formed them on the regimental colors near the Stone House intersection. He sat on his horse and stared back at the battle "as if paralyzed," recalled an onlooker, while his small band "stood under the colors silent as statues, gazing vacantly at the tumultuous concourse trudging by."[19]

A few minutes after Hood launched his assault, a courier from Longstreet summoned Hood to his commander's headquarters. The Texan galloped at full speed to see his general. Longstreet instructed Hood "not to allow his division to move so far forward as to throw itself beyond the prompt support of the troops he had ordered to the front." Longstreet knew that coordination was the key to victory and did not want Hood to get carried away because of his impetuousness. Although Hood rode back to the front as fast as his horse could take him, Longstreet's fear had already become a reality. The Texans had surged ahead of the supporting troops, and Hood did not reach his brigade until it was too late to preserve the attack's overall coordination. While the Texas Brigade had scored a smashing tactical success against Warren, their rapid advance disrupted the timing of Longstreet's attack. "We should have halted at this branch and waited for support," recalled a soldier of the 4th Texas, "but not being cognizant of the order, we pushed on up the slope."[20]

DOGAN RIDGE

Hood's lightning-quick attack confirmed Franz Sigel's concern for the Federal left flank. Hearing the incessant volleys of musketry, the German ordered Brig. Gen. Robert H. Milroy's brigade to McLean's aid. Milroy's West Virginians and Ohioans had previously deployed across the Warrenton Turnpike at the base of Dogan Ridge to rally Porter's defeated troops. Upon receiving Sigel's order, Milroy put his brigade in motion toward Chinn Ridge, and then he went to Sigel for precise information on the desired position. Sigel told Milroy to take position on a wooded portion of Chinn Ridge to McLean's left, after which Milroy dashed back to his brigade. Upon reaching his command, Milroy was informed by an aide that Colonel Ruggles of Pope's staff was looking for him. Wasting no time, Milroy ordered his lead regiment toward the wooded stretch of Chinn Ridge before riding back to see Ruggles. The staff officer ordered Milroy to move his brigade to Henry Hill. Milroy immediately recalled his brigade and marched toward the hill. By altering Milroy's orders, Pope had thwarted Sigel's attempt to reinforce McLean on Chinn Ridge. If Milroy's brigade had come to McLean's assistance as Sigel ordered, it might have altered the outcome of the fighting on Chinn Ridge, as he would have been in place when the Confederates first appeared. Instead, for a critical amount of time McLean would fight unsupported.[21]

WARRENTON TURNPIKE, NEAR DOGAN RIDGE

The thunderous Confederate volleys south of the turnpike had likewise alerted McDowell to his folly of removing Reynolds's division from Chinn Ridge. Hoping to retrieve the situation, McDowell dashed after the Pennsylvanians, meeting Col. Martin Hardin, the commander of Reynolds's rear brigade. Hardin saw McDowell shortly after Hood's attack began and thought him to be "the most excited officer" the colonel had ever encountered during the war. McDowell halted Hardin's brigade and two Pennsylvania batteries, ordering them into position on a hill immediately east of Young's Branch, behind Warren's position. One Pennsylvanian who overheard McDowell's words turned to his fellow Reserves and loudly exclaimed, "Don't the damned fool see that when we get down there, the Johnnies in the woods will surely flank us?" McDowell knew well the fate that awaited the Pennsylvanians; nevertheless, he had no choice but to sacrifice some of his troops to buy time for the army.[22]

Hardin and battery commander Capt. Mark Kerns rode ahead of their units to the crest of the hill. There, they saw Warren's brigade breaking to the rear. Captain Kerns scanned the landscape and declared that he would plant his battery on the spot where he now stood. Hardin galloped back to his brigade and shouted, "Left into line, wheel!" By the time Hardin's Pennsylvanians reached the hill, Kerns had deployed his four 10-pounder Parrott guns, but Warren's fugitives limited his ability to fire. Hardin deployed his brigade in two lines of battle to Kerns's left. Capt. John Simpson deployed his Pennsylvania battery somewhere on the hill with Hardin and experienced similar problems.[23]

The Zouaves finally cleared Kerns's front, and the Pennsylvania gunners pounded Hood's men when they reached the foot of the hill. Warren rallied what few survivors he could on the Pennsylvanians' battle line and assisted in slowing the Confederate assault. The initial shock of the Pennsylvanians' fresh resistance stalled Hood's attacking brigade. The sudden Federal resistance prompted Captain Sellers to halt the Texas Brigade and attempt to coordinate its further advance as Longstreet desired. Because of the death of Lieutenant Colonel Upton, however, the right wing of Colonel Robertson's 5th Texas had not received the order to halt and continued its rapid advance. This proved fortuitous, as the 5th Texas's right wing flanked the left of Hardin's brigade. Robertson immediately recognized the advantage gained and followed it up with the balance of the 5th Texas. The Hampton Legion and 18th Georgia moved forward, and charged Hardin's Pennsylvanians with a shout. Hardin fell seriously wounded but urged his men to hold out until reinforcements arrived. The Pennsylvania Reserves soon streamed rearward in confusion, however, having been overwhelmed on their left.

Simpson's battery limbered up and joined the infantry in headlong retreat, leaving Captain Kerns and his artillerists to fend for themselves.[24]

On Hood's left flank, Lt. Col. B. F. Carter's 4th Texas charged up the slope from Young's Branch toward the three left guns of Kerns's battery. As he and his Texans covered the hundred yards between Young's Branch and the guns, the Pennsylvanians greeted the Southerners with "a terrific fire of grape, canister and musketry, as Carter reported." Under this lethal barrage, Carter's regiment lost twenty-two men killed and sixty-six wounded. Nevertheless, the Texans kept going, firing as they went. Their fire killed three Pennsylvanians and wounded twenty-three others from the battery. Confederate missiles struck Kerns in the head and arm, severely wounding him. The Pennsylvanians placed Kerns and two other wounded men on a caisson to carry them out, but a "heavy shell struck the caisson battering it to pieces." The surviving Pennsylvania gunners stayed at their pieces and fired at the Confederates until the 4th Texas approached to within twenty paces. Then, with almost a quarter of the battery's men lying dead or wounded on the ground, the gunners abandoned their pieces and joined the Pennsylvania Reserves in headlong retreat. The Texans surged over the battery and captured four guns. They found Captain Kerns lying mortally wounded near his battery. The dying Pennsylvanian told the Texans, "I have promised to drive you back, or die under my guns, and I have kept my word."[25]

From the ravine behind Kerns's position, Col. John C. Lee of the 55th Ohio saw large bodies of Federal troops retreating past his right flank. Lee, an attorney from Tiffin, Ohio, spurred his horse and galloped toward the retreating men to learn the reason for their retrograde movement. The beaten Federals excitedly told Lee that the Confederates were advancing down the Warrenton Turnpike. Lee instantly recognized the gravity of the situation, galloped back to the 55th Ohio, and ordered an advance. Lee's Buckeyes ascended to the crest of the hill, where they encountered the retreating Pennsylvanians. One Ohioan wrote that the Pennsylvanians "came back, pell-mell, trying to run through our line of battle in their retreat or rather *skedaddle,* but we kept punching them back with the butt of our muskets." The Ohioans fired several volleys into the 4th Texas, but the confusion caused by the

EVANS AND KEMPER STRIKE CHINN RIDGE

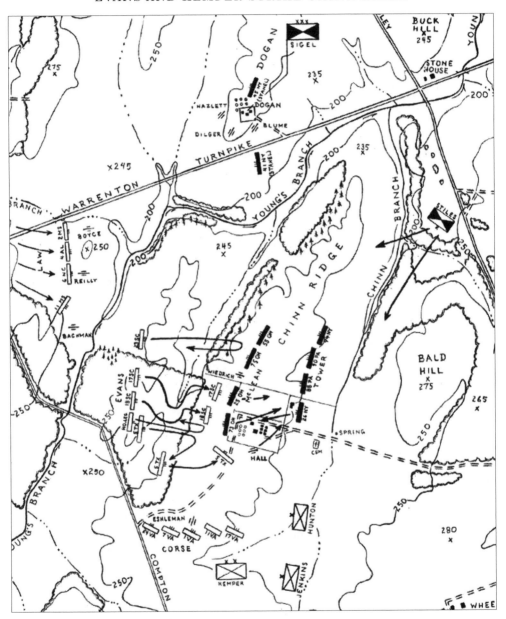

John C. McAnaw

retreating Pennsylvanians prevented them from effectively engaging the Southerners. To make matters worse, Simpson's battery dashed through the 55th Ohio, throwing it into temporary disorder.[26]

Colonel Lee quickly realized that one regiment could not salvage the situation around Kerns's battery. "With this mass pressing against us it was impossible to fire," reported Lee, "and, being wholly unsupported, the battalion was faced by the rear rank and moved rapidly over to the ridge behind us." There, Lee reformed the 55th Ohio under the long-distance musketry of the 4th Texas. With order restored, the 55th Ohio moved by the left flank to rejoin McLean's brigade farther south on Chinn Ridge.[27]

Meanwhile, the Pennsylvania Reserves had retreated toward the Warrenton Turnpike while Hood's men inclined their advance slightly to their right. Cpl. Abraham Rudisill of Kerns's battery ran through the woods with the mob of Pennsylvanians, the Texans following close behind. Rudisill and company soon found themselves caught between the Texans and the 55th Ohio, with many Pennsylvanians falling victim to friendly fire. Rudisill passed safely through the battle line of the 55th Ohio, slowing down to a walk. Crossing a ravine and ascending Chinn Ridge, Rudisill heard someone shout, "Get out of the way!" Not realizing that he was the intended recipient of the warning, Rudisill continued up the ridge, course unaltered, until a comrade yelled, "Get out of the way quick! They are going to fire!" Rudisill suddenly found himself staring down the barrel of a loaded cannon. He barely managed two quick sidesteps before the gunner pulled the lanyard, sending the load flying past the stunned Rudisill's head.[28]

On Chinn Ridge, McLean's brigade occupied the fields of Hazel Plain, the Chinn family's farmstead. The Chinn House had witnessed the closing scenes of the Battle of First Manassas and served as a field hospital in 1861. It rested in the middle of a large, rolling field enclosed by a rail fence. This enclosure formed a square that another fence divided into halves. The eastern half contained the Chinn House and several outbuildings, most notably a structure that doubled as a chicken coop and woodshed. A lane running from the Sudley Road to Compton Road passed through this same section. To the west of their house, the Chinn family had cultivated an apple orchard. The slave quarters and summer kitchen lay on the northeast side of their home, opposite the woodshed. The other half of the enclosed area consisted of a garden.

A hardwood forest bordered Hazel Plain to the west and extended to Young's Branch. Open pastures rolling toward the Warrenton Turnpike dominated the area north of the enclosed field. Pasturelands also bordered the southern edge of the enclosed field. To the east, the ground sloped quickly to form a hollow between Chinn Ridge and Bald Hill. Chinn Branch, a steep-banked stream fed by Chinn Spring, meandered through this vale.[29]

Col. Nathaniel C. McLean formed his battle line fronting westward. He anchored his left flank with the 73rd Ohio. The hardwood forest lay only ninety yards in front of the 73rd Ohio, and the Chinn House sat to its left rear. The 25th Ohio deployed next and extended McLean's line northward, facing cleared fields and pine thickets to the west. Wiedrich's battery deployed slightly in advance of the infantry on the right flank of the 25th Ohio. The 75th Ohio extended the line farther northward into the open pastures of Hazel Plain. The only combat-ready Federals standing between Longstreet and Bull Run, these Ohioans constituted the Union's sole line of defense on Chinn Ridge. It would be up to McLean's Buckeyes to buy enough time for Pope to shift units to Henry Hill and save his army from irreparable harm.[30]

From the heights of Chinn Ridge, McLean and his men had watched Hood's brigade destroy Warren's Zouaves. They plainly saw the swift defeat of Colonel Hardin's Pennsylvania Reserves and the capture of Kerns's battery. The latter action had occurred on a knoll to the right front of McLean's position. When Hood's men appeared on that knoll, McLean ordered Captain Wiedrich to open fire with his four 10-pounder Parrott guns. Wiedrich's German gunners sailed their missiles into Hood's victory-seeking Confederates, who recalled advancing through "a rain of shell." With the exception of the 1st Texas, Hood's brigade descended the hill to a ravine separating Chinn Ridge from the hill where Kerns had deployed. There, the Texans halted to wait for reinforcements.

The Southern officers had trouble restraining their jubilant men, and many Texans, Georgians, and South Carolinians crawled to the top of the ravine's eastern slope, where they fired at the 75th Ohio on McLean's right flank. The Southerners then returned to the gully to load and then crawled back up to fire once more. Others took advantage of the halt, and simply lay down to catch their breath and rest.[31]

Meanwhile, Colonel Work of the wayward 1st Texas learned that the balance of the brigade had crossed Young's Branch and ascended the hill beyond. Work hurried the 1st Texas across the branch and marched up the hill where Kerns's abandoned guns sat. There, the 1st Texas had encountered the heavy fire from Dogan Ridge where the Union batteries were posted, including that of his nemesis Cog Hazlett. To avoid needless slaughter, Work placed the 1st Texas in a slight depression that sheltered it from the Union artillery projectiles.

Work heard heavy rifle fire emanating from the ravine in front of him but failed to see the 4th Texas, owing to the lay of the ground. An officer of Hood's staff appeared on the scene, exclaiming that "all of the regiments of the brigade were down in the hollow, were hard pressed and needed assistance." Work promptly ordered the 1st Texas forward to rejoin the brigade. Just as he gave the command to advance, Captain Sellers, the nominal brigade commander, appeared on the scene and ordered Work to take his regiment under cover. Before Work could act, Sellers impatiently ordered the 1st Texas to about-face. The 1st Texas then proceeded to march back to Young's Branch, where it sat for the rest of the battle.[32]

Back in the hollow, Col. Jerome B. Robertson of the 5th Texas surveyed the situation on Chinn Ridge and realized that McLean's line outflanked the Texans on the right by several hundred yards, with the Federal batteries at Dogan Ridge pounding his northern flank. Robertson was a man of action, having gone in 1836 to Texas, where he served as a captain in the Army of the Republic of Texas. In 1837 he married Mary Elizabeth Cummins, and returned to Texas with her and several relatives, settling on the Brazos River. He gained additional military experience in repelling invasions by the Mexican Army in 1842 and served in the Texas legislature.

When Robertson was unable to find either Hood or Sellers, the Texan galloped down the battle line to his left and conferred with Col. William T.

Wofford of the 18th Georgia and Lt. Col. Martin W. Gary of the Hampton Legion. Robertson suggested that the three officers file their regiments up the ravine to their right, where a hardwood forest would provide shelter from the Union fire. The two officers assented, and Robertson returned to his 5th Texas.[33]

At the opposite end of Hood's line, Lieutenant Colonel Carter of the 4th Texas assessed the situation in his sector. He saw reinforcements that Sigel had belatedly sent marching from Dogan Ridge to the south side of the Warrenton Turnpike. Carter then looked to his right and saw Wofford's 18th Georgia moving away from the 4th Texas toward the hardwoods. Carter sent Wofford a staff officer, who informed the Georgian of the dire situation in which the 4th Texas now found itself. Wofford replied that the 18th Georgia could be of no assistance as it was going to the right with Robertson. Why Robertson, Wofford, and Gary did not include Carter in their conference or inform him of their intentions before moving is not known. Regardless, this incident underscored the lack of guidance and coordination the Texans received at the brigade level. This dearth of leadership prompted Robertson to complain in his official report, "The separation of the regiments of the brigade during the battle . . . demonstrated the absolute necessity of having brigade commanders present with brigades at all times during the engagement."[34]

The 4th Texas remained under the enfilading fire from Dogan Ridge a few minutes more, in hopes that the 1st Texas would come to its support. Finally, the unsupported Texans retired to a dry creek bed fifty yards to their rear. There, the 4th Texas still suffered under a heavy crossfire from the Union batteries on Dogan Ridge. At length, Carter concluded that no support was forthcoming and pulled the 4th Texas back to Young's Branch. As the 4th Texas passed by Kerns's guns, Pvt. Granfield H. Crozier was lying on the ground with a broken arm and saw his comrades marching to the rear. He grew concerned at the sight of his regiment falling back from the front for he "had never seen Texans retreat before." He asked an officer what was wrong, and a cocky lieutenant reassured Crozier, telling him "they had whipped the Yankees and had just come back to the shade to rest." The 4th

Texas was done fighting for the day, though the battle had only begun.[35]

While Carter pulled back, the 5th Texas, Hampton Legion, and 18th Georgia filed up the ravine toward the hardwoods. Shortly before the Southerners moved out, Col. Orland Smith of the 73rd Ohio sent Capt. Luther Buckwalter's company into the woods as skirmishers. The 5th Texas and Hampton Legion entered the woods and encountered the lone company of Ohioans. Both sides fired briefly, but Confederate numbers prevailed and the Ohioans fell back on their main battle line. The 5th Texas moved far enough into the woods for the Hampton Legion and 18th Georgia to likewise gain the shelter of the trees. During this encounter, a Texan fell mortally wounded and appealed to a passing comrade for aid. The comrade did not stop; his strict duty to his regiment and "country drove back the generous impulse of nature to aid" the disabled Texan.[36]

Out on the Warrenton Turnpike, General Longstreet witnessed the devastating impact that the Union batteries on Dogan Ridge had had on his attack. Longstreet ordered Maj. Bushrod W. Frobel, commander of Hood's divisional artillery, "to proceed down the turnpike" and to open fire on the Federal batteries posted in the orchard near the Dogan house. Frobel's three batteries initially went into position on the north side of the Warrenton Turnpike, where the Federal artillery opened a "fearful fire" on the Southerners. Still the more numerous, Federal rifled cannon continued to deal their deadly projectiles. To silence these batteries, Longstreet required Jackson's assistance. If Jackson's wing advanced, it would draw the attention of the Federal artillerists from Longstreet's wing and allow him to sweep up the turnpike. Longstreet waited, but the hoped-for movement by Jackson failed to manifest itself in a timely fashion, as Stonewall's men needed to ready themselves for combat after dispatching Porter's attack.[37]

As the crescendo of battle grew on Chinn Ridge, Longstreet realized that Federal resistance was stiffening and ordered Brig. Gen. Cadmus M. Wilcox of Alabama to bring his entire division to Hood's aid on the south side of the Warrenton Turnpike. Previously, when Porter's attack began to recede, Wilcox had advanced his division in pursuit of the retreating Federals, hoping to cut them off, but halted after a short distance to await support. When

Wilcox received Longstreet's initial orders to counterattack, the Alabaman's division moved across an open field and entered the Groveton woods under "a terrific artillery fire." Reaching the opposite edge of the woods, Wilcox found his division "broken and somewhat scattered" and saw the formidable Federal artillery drawn up on Dogan Ridge. There his division remained, pinned down by the Federal batteries, until Longstreet directed Wilcox to Chinn Ridge.[38]

From the start, the movement to Chinn Ridge went awry for Wilcox. Longstreet intended for Wilcox to bring his entire division to Hood's support, yet the Alabaman brought only his own brigade. Both Wilcox and Brig. Gen. Winfield Scott Featherston (who remained behind in command of Wilcox's two remaining brigades north of the road) reported that Wilcox received orders to take only his brigade. Either Wilcox botched the order or the staff officer bringing Longstreet's instructions failed to deliver them as Longstreet intended. Either way, this miscommunication prevented Longstreet's wishes from becoming a reality on the battlefield. The subsequent lack of movement by Featherston's brigades likely delayed Jackson's joining the attack, as Lee had instructed Stonewall to move forward to support Longstreet's left flank. When it did not move forward in a timely manner, neither did Jackson. To make matters worse, Wilcox's lone brigade foundered about for at least thirty minutes and failed to locate Hood even after it crossed to the south side of the Warrenton Turnpike. As a result, Wilcox's troops played no meaningful role in the coming battle, much to Longstreet's chagrin.[39]

Three

"PERFECT STORMS OF BULLETS"

COL. WILLIAM T. WOFFORD and Lt. Col. Martin W. Gary wasted no time sending the 18th Georgia and Hampton Legion back into action. Wofford, a Mexican War veteran and native Georgian, looked to press the attack against the Federals on Chinn Ridge. However, the lack of an overall guiding hand in Hood's brigade limited their chances for success from the outset; while the Georgians and South Carolinians attacked, Robertson rested the 5th Texas in the woods. This lack of coordination resulted from Hood's failure to remain with the brigade or to appoint a competent acting commander of sufficient rank. Hood's man on the scene, Captain Sellers, who had already removed the 1st Texas from the battle, did little to coordinate the movements of Hood's brigade. As a result, the 18th Georgia and Hampton Legion attacked McLean's brigade without support. It was just the sort of situation that Longstreet had hoped to avoid.

Wofford halted the 18th Georgia as soon as the trees concealed its left flank. He then advanced through the woods in line of battle toward Wiedrich's battery. The Georgians and South Carolinians charged over a slight declivity to within forty yards of the German's guns. Wiedrich's gunners rammed rounds of canister into their guns and opened fire on the approaching Southerners. The 25th and 75th Ohio fired their rifles unmercifully into the Confederates, cutting them down by the score. The 18th Georgia's color-sergeant carried the regiment's battle flag to "the mouth of the guns," where he received two "painful" wounds. As soon as the colors hit the ground, another Georgian retrieved them and flaunted the banner at the Ohioans. He and one other fell wounded before the flag was saved. After the battle, soldiers of the 18th Georgia counted seventeen bullet holes in their battle flag, and another bullet had splintered the staff.[1]

The Hampton Legion emerged from the woods on the right flank of Wofford's 18th Georgia but fell back into the woods after absorbing several volleys from 25th Ohio. Wofford's rugged Georgians fired several volleys back at the Ohioans. The exposed Southerners provided ample targets for the Federals on the ridge. "Now was our game," declared Lt. George B. Fox of the 75th Ohio, "a few volleys and they just more than scattered." As the Georgians and South Carolinians withdrew from the combat, Brig. Gen. Nathan Evans's South Carolinians passed by on their way to the front. Wofford and Gary continued rearward and led the bloodied remnants of their regiments to Young's Branch, where they found Captain Sellers resting the 1st and 4th Texas. This sight must have infuriated Wofford, who complained about the lack of support in his official report.[2]

While McLean battled Wofford and Gary, a large body of troops emerged from the woods a half mile out on the Ohioans' left flank. These troops belonged to Brig. Gen. James L. Kemper's division. Kemper's men had been resting along the banks of Young's Branch, near the William Lewis Farm, when the order to advance came. Like every other Confederate command, this division trailed behind Hood's surging brigade. Kemper moved forward in sync with Evans's brigade. Kemper's division consisted of three brigades moving in two lines of battle. Brig. Gen. Micah Jenkins's South Carolinians held the right of the front line, with Col. Eppa Hunton's Virginians manning the left. Col. Montgomery D. Corse's Virginians marched in line of battle 250 yards behind Hunton's brigade.

As soon as Kemper's front line began to advance, he dashed back to Corse's brigade, shouting, "Hurry up, men, hurry up! I have seen the whole fight. The enemy is in full retreat, and if you don't hurry up, you won't even get to see their backs." As Kemper spoke, the sound of rapidly increasing musketry mocked his words. One wag chimed in, "Well, General, I guess we will get to see their bellies," eliciting laughter from the Virginians.[3]

Kemper's division descended from the heights near the Lewis farm and crossed Young's Branch, entering a hardwood grove east of the stream. Kemper's left flank continued through the woods that gave way to open fields in Jenkins's front. The division ultimately emerged about a half mile out on the left flank of McLean's brigade, where it was ideally poised to wreak havoc on the Federals if properly handled. As the division appeared on the scene, Hunton's men looked to their left and saw Hood's battle flags fall to the ground repeatedly in front of McLean's Ohioans. The time was ripe for Kemper, Hunton, and Jenkins to quickly change front and sweep McLean off Chinn Ridge. Such action would have doomed McLean's stand then and there.

It was not to be. Hunton's men flushed a small body of Federals out of the woods. The Virginians grew excited at the sight of retreating Yankees and pressed on in pursuit, failing to perceive the opportunity on Chinn Ridge. Hunton reported, "The ardor of the troops at this time was very great." He admitted experiencing "some difficulty in holding them well in hand." Such an admission in his report more likely meant that he probably lost all control of the men. The brigade did not halt until reaching Chinn Branch, and even then it took a while to regain control. For the time being, Hunton's brigade (and Jenkins's) did not factor into the fight for Chinn Ridge. Beyond exhorting the men to hurry forward, Kemper apparently did little to rectify the situation and exercised little effective control of his division.[4]

In the Federal ranks on Chinn Ridge, Maj. Samuel Hurst of the 73rd Ohio noticed Kemper's division emerging from the woods off to McLean's left flank. Hurst warned his regimental commander, Col. Orland Smith, of the development; Smith then promptly relayed the intelligence to McLean. McLean initially ordered Captain Wiedrich to "turn two pieces of artillery upon them." But before Wiedrich fired the guns, "someone who professed to know" assured McLean that Kemper's battalions were Federal reinforcements moving to support the Ohioans' left flank. Accepting this assessment at face value, McLean countermanded Wiedrich's orders and "assured" the officers of the 73rd Ohio that the troops moving toward them were friends. Only the confusion in Kemper's front line granted McLean a temporary reprieve, giving the Buckeyes the time needed to deal exclusively with Evans's South Carolinians and the 5th Texas.[5]

The "someone who professed to know" was an officer from the right wing of the army who McLean did not identify by name in his after-action report. One likely candidate was his division commander, Brig. Gen. Robert Schenck, who had arrived on Chinn Ridge shortly after the combat began. Whoever it was must have known that Sigel had ordered Milroy's brigade to McLean's support. The last that this unnamed officer knew of Milroy was that he was moving south through the woods along Chinn Branch in McLean's rear. The officer could not have known that Pope had altered Milroy's orders. So, the "someone" had assumed that the troops he saw moving toward McLean's left were Milroy's. McLean's "first and better judgment" had been right on target, but the fog of war had obscured reality.[6]

At some point during the combat on Chinn Ridge, Capt. James H. Cooper's Battery B, 1st Pennsylvania Light Artillery, arrived and went into position off to McLean's left flank near the Chinn House. Although its arrival went unnoticed by the Ohioans amid the smoke and din of battle, Confederate sources clearly indicate the presence of a second battery on McLean's left near the Chinn House. Once in position, Cooper's Pennsylvanians greeted the Texans and South Carolinians with shell and canister, slowing the gray tide.[7]

Brig. Gen. Nathan George "Shanks" Evans was back on the plains of Manassas where in 1861 he had become one of the Confederacy's first heroes. Evans had graduated from West Point in 1848 with notable cavalry officers William E. "Grumble" Jones and John Buford. He had earned a reputation for bravery and fearlessness during the Plains Indian Wars, and had once killed two Kiowa warriors in hand-to-hand combat during an engagement in Kansas. Evans had married a sister of the Hampton Legion's Lieutenant Colonel Gary in 1860 and remained in the U.S. Army until resigning in February 1861 because of the secession crisis.

In the first year of the war, Evans demonstrated as much tactical ability as any other officer in the Confederate service. At First Manassas, he learned of the Federal flanking movement and rushed his small brigade to Matthew's

Hill, where he fought a brilliant delaying action that laid the foundation for a Confederate victory. If not for Evans's rapid response to the Federal flanking attack, Stonewall Jackson would not have had the opportunity to immortalize his name on Henry Hill. For the bold stand on Matthew's Hill, Gen. Pierre G. T. Beauregard commended Evans's "dauntless conduct and imperturbable coolness," while Gen. Joseph E. Johnston cited the South Carolinian's "skill and unshrinking courage." In October 1861 Evans shattered a Union reconnaissance force near Leesburg at the battle of Ball's Bluff. His troops inflicted over 900 casualties (out of 1,700 Federals engaged) while losing only 150 men.

For his actions, Evans received a promotion to brigadier general and command of a new brigade from the South Carolina coast. On June 15, 1862, Evans assumed command of the Confederate defenses of James Island, a key link in the defenses of Charleston. The following day, troops from Evans's command repelled a Federal attack at the battle of Secessionville, inflicting almost 700 Union casualties with the loss of only 200 Confederates.

Although Evans demonstrated tactical brilliance and personal bravery, his fondness for alcohol severely hampered his chances for promotion and often impaired his effectiveness as an officer. He was famous throughout the army for having a Prussian orderly who kept a gallon keg of whiskey, affectionately referred to by Evans as his Barrelita, close at hand. A member of his staff remarked, "If Nathan is the bravest and best General in the C. S., if not the world, he is at the same time about the best drinker, the most eloquent swearer (I should say voluble) and the most magnificent bragger I ever saw."[8]

Evans also possessed a penchant for straight, sometimes belligerent talk. Once, a young, arrogant man smoking a cigar approached Evans and postulated, "What would you do if you were I, and I were you?" Evans sized up the upstart and noticed that he sported a gold-headed walking stick and wore his watch outside his coat for all to see. Evans retorted, "Well, if I were you, I would throw away that vile cigar, cut up my cane for firewood, wear my watch chain underneath my coat, and stay at home nights and pray for brains."[9]

When Evans returned to Virginia in July 1862 with his brigade, he found that much had changed. Johnston and Beauregard had long since departed from the Confederate army in Virginia. Junior officers who had not even served at First Manassas now commanded divisions, but officially Evans still led only a brigade. All in all, Evans probably felt out of place in Robert E. Lee's Army of Northern Virginia. Its officers in turn found Evans "difficult to manage." Nevertheless, Longstreet placed Evans in command of a division comprising his own brigade and Hood's division at noon on August 30. Although Evans commanded the division, Longstreet conferred with Hood when the time to attack arrived, effectively removing the swaggering South Carolinian from the chain of command. Longstreet never explained his reasoning, but in all likelihood, his confidence in Hood and Evans's reputation for drinking drove his actions.[10]

Evans's brigade had initially occupied a wood line located two hundred yards behind the Texas Brigade's original position on the Cundiffe Farm. The South Carolinians grew anxious waiting in the woods and their tension mounted, for Second Manassas was their first major battle. Evans's men had previously served along the South Carolina coast and had only arrived in Virginia in mid-July. Col. Peter F. Stevens, a former superintendent of the Citadel, deployed the brigade into line of battle with the 23rd South Carolina on the left, the 17th and 18th regiments in the center, and the Holcombe Legion on the right flank. Shortly after four o'clock, Evans's brigade stepped out of the woods and followed in the wake of the surging Texas Brigade.

Evans's brigade had advanced only fifty yards when the Union artillery on Dogan Ridge homed in on the South Carolinians. Col. Henry L. Benbow, commander of the 23rd South Carolina, fell seriously wounded, and Lt. Col. John M. Roberts immediately assumed command. Colonel Stevens galloped out in front of the shaken 23rd, calming the men and renewing the advance. Still, the fire of the Union artillery on Dogan Ridge forced the South Carolinians to oblique their advance southward.

The South Carolinians passed through the woods near Lewis Lane, over the fields strewn with the dead and wounded Zouaves of Warren's brigade. The South Carolinians, clad in relatively new uniforms, descended the slope toward Young's Branch in excellent order. Resting near the creek, a member of the 4th Texas described Evans's brigade "as pretty a sight" as the Texan ever saw. Dirtying their uniforms, the South Carolinians sliced through Young's Branch and entered the woods behind the 18th Georgia, Hampton Legion, and 5th Texas. Despite the cover offered by the trees, the Union artillery on Dogan and Chinn ridges continuously pounded the South Carolinians. Evans and Stevens saw the flash of Wiedrich's and Cooper's guns firing atop Chinn Ridge and shouted, "Lie down!" The men had barely hit the ground before the iron balls whizzed overhead, slicing through the timber. The South Carolinians then rose up and treaded through the woods, sometimes halting and lying down to avoid the Union artillery fire, only to rise up and move forward once again.[11]

Evans's brigade emerged from the woods on Chinn Ridge so closely behind the 18th Georgia and Hampton Legion that the Ohioans believed the Confederates were attacking in columns. Evans's brigade moved through the woods and entered the open ground in McLean's front. The wood line ran obliquely across the front of Evans's brigade. The trees on Evans's right flank extended closer to McLean's position than those on the South Carolinians' left. This provided the South Carolinians on the right with cover for a longer period of time during their advance. Consequently, Evans's units seemed to emerge from the woods individually, with his left flank entering the open ground first.[12]

As Evans's brigade approached Chinn Ridge, Colonel Lee's 55th Ohio filed into line on McLean's right flank, adding desperately needed firepower to the Union effort. When the 23rd South Carolina neared the tree line, a Federal Minié ball knocked Lieutenant Colonel Roberts off his horse, mortally wounding him. Command of the Coast Rangers, as the 23rd South Carolina was also known, passed to twenty-three-year-old Maj. John Marshall Whilden of Charleston. Whilden had attended King's Mountain Military School, where he became a protégé of future Confederate general Micah Jenkins. After completing that curriculum, the young Charlestonian attended the South Carolina Military Academy at the Citadel, from which he graduated in 1861.

As a cadet captain, Whilden had commanded the battery that fired on the *Star of the West* as it attempted to reinforce Fort Sumter in Charleston

Harbor. He also participated in the bombardment of that Federal installation. Three months later, Whilden followed his mentor, now colonel Micah Jenkins, to Virginia, where he fought as a lieutenant in the 5th South Carolina Infantry at First Manassas. Although young, Maj. John Marshall Whilden possessed the character and credentials that marked him as a potential star in the Confederate army.

As the 23rd South Carolina entered the open ground in front of Chinn Ridge (slightly to the left of where the 18th Georgia fought), Whilden ordered a charge, but the 55th and 75th Ohio fired a telling volley that brought down the Coast Rangers' flag bearer. Whilden snatched up the fallen colors and waved them overhead. Rallying his troops, he attempted to press the attack, but the Buckeyes smothered it with their musketry. Still brandishing his colors, young Major Whilden rallied some of his men and dashed toward McLean's position. Five bullets ripped into Whilden, mortally wounding him. The rest of the 23rd South Carolina stumbled back into the woods, having lost 149 out of 250 who went into action.[13]

The appearance of the 23rd South Carolina also drew more unwanted attention from the Union artillery on Dogan Ridge. The 17th and 18th South Carolina encountered a tempest of lead and iron as they neared the edge of the trees. Bullets and shells that overshot the 23rd South Carolina struck the 17th and 18th regiments on the left flank. To avoid this metallic storm, the 17th and 18th South Carolina inclined farther to the right and remained under the cover of the woods.[14]

On Evans's right flank, the Holcombe Legion advanced through the woods and passed over the left flank of the prone 5th Texas. The legion's officers shouted the command forward, and the Texans mistook the command for them and, as Robertson reported, "became considerably scattered by intermixing" with the Holcombe Legion. With the 17th and 18th South Carolina stacked up behind the legion, a powerful throng of South Carolinians and Texans trudged through the woods toward McLean's left flank.[15]

Col. Orland Smith, a superintendent and auditor for the Marietta and Cincinnati Railroad in civilian life, rode along the 73rd Ohio's battle line and ordered the men to hold their fire until he gave the command. "Yelling like demons," the South Carolinians and Texans rushed out of the woods, and Smith shouted, "Fire!" The 73rd Ohio's Maj. Samuel Hurst expounded, "We poured such a murderous volley into them that they retreated to the cover of the woods again." Cooper's Pennsylvania gunners lashed out at the Southerners with a lethal blast of canister. The Ohioans cheered as the Texans and South Carolinians hurried back to the woods. From the wood line, many of the South Carolinians and Texans returned fire at the Ohioans. Hurst recalled, "It was the first real, earnest, open-field, line of battle fighting we had done, and the regiment seemed determined to acquit itself well." Among the soldiers fighting with the 73rd Ohio stood George Nixon, great-grandfather of future president Richard M. Nixon. He served with the unit until falling mortally wounded at Gettysburg.[16]

The 73rd Ohio's musketry wreaked havoc among the Confederate ranks. The Holcombe Legion lost both its lieutenant colonel and major. It suffered so severely that a lieutenant commanded the legion by the battle's end. One legionnaire wrote,

> I never conceived that a fire could be so heavy. I realized the truth of the expression that, "the air was heavy with balls." It seemed to me that every square inch of a man's body might have been hit. The balls all seemed, too, to cut low. . . . As we advanced towards the enemy under this terrific fire we had to pass through a very thick wood—we were a mere mob. There stood the enemy, drawn up in beautiful line, and had they only advanced, they could have routed and captured us.[17]

But McLean had more to worry about than merely the Confederates in his immediate front. With Kemper's division menacingly lurking beyond McLean's left flank, his men gave little thought to advancing at the time but realized the severity of combat was about to increase.

Before Kemper's foot soldiers hit McLean, the Confederate artillery made its presence known. Confederate cavalry commander Maj. Gen. Jeb Stuart advanced every battery that he could find. Under the immediate guidance of Col. Thomas Rosser, the guns galloped forward on the extreme right of the Confederate army to enfilade the Union troops. Rosser deployed Capt. Benjamin F. Eshleman's company of the Washington Artillery on a slight eminence to the left front of McLean's brigade. From this position, the Louisianans' fire enfiladed the left flank of McLean's brigade. Major Hurst of the 73rd Ohio wrote, "The shot and shell came plowing down our line." Any lingering doubt concerning the identity of the forces moving on McLean's left vanished with the crash of the first shell.[18]

In the woods in front of the Ohioans, the officers of Evans's brigade worked desperately to regain control of their units amid the confusion. Colonel Robertson pulled the 5th Texas out of the mob and rallied it off to the right of Evans's South Carolinians. Colonel Stevens attempted to advance Evans's men, but in the din of battle, he could not make himself be understood. Stevens "found the line halted and staggering under the murderous fire of grape, canister and musketry." He shouted the command "charge" but "found it impossible for officers to make themselves be obeyed" as the Confederates struggled amid the storm of lead hurled at them by McLean's Ohioans.[19]

In an attempt to urge the brigade ahead, Stevens gradually ended up on the extreme right of the line. There, he spotted Colonel Robertson's 5th Texas "moving in splendid order." The Texans advanced and veered to the right, away from Evans's brigade. As Stevens told it, he rode to Robertson and directed the Texans to support Evans's beleaguered men. Although Robertson made no mention of Stevens in his report, the Texans marched out of the woods to where they were needed most.[20]

While Stevens rode after the Texans, the regimental commanders of Evans's brigade sorted their jumbled ranks out and reentered the fray. In front of McLean's left wing, Col. John Hugh Means, commander of the 17th South Carolina, extricated his unit from the confusion. Means saw General Hood arrive on the scene and rode up to him, requesting orders. Hood directed Means to seize Wiedrich's battery, which was only a hundred yards away. These orders suited the fiery South Carolinian well, for he had long sought an opportunity to cross swords with the hated Yankees.

South Carolinians had elected Means their governor in 1850. Even then, Means had championed South Carolina's withdrawal from the Union. During his term, Means increased the Palmetto State's military expenditures and improved the militia system in expectation of war with the North. But Means proved too venomous even for South Carolina and lost his bid for reelection in 1852. Retiring from politics, he returned to his plantation in South Carolina's Fairfield District until 1860, when he served as a delegate to South Carolina's secession convention. Unlike many fire-eaters and abolitionists, Means would fight the war he had so ardently advocated, although his advanced age would have permitted him to avoid military service without shame. He dutifully enlisted in the 17th South Carolina Infantry as a private. Recognizing Means's leadership ability, the men of the 17th South Carolina elected him colonel.[21]

The tempestuous Means marched the 17th South Carolina by the left flank out of the woods and into the field. Once in the open, Means gallantly cheered his men, crying out, "Push on, my boys! Push on!" In Hood's words, the 17th "boldly dashed forward" toward the 25th Ohio, which greeted the South Carolinians with a volley. Colonel Means toppled from his saddle mortally wounded, and his men faltered under the intense rifle fire. An officer of the 25th Ohio vividly recalled,

> They marched up like mad men, not a charge, but marched up in solid column without firing a shot. As fast as one regiment was mowed down like grass by the scythe, another stepped up in its place. I know that our brigade killed and wounded more than their own number.[22]

Col. J. M. Gadberry guided the 18th South Carolina out of the chaos in the timber on Means's right flank. The South Carolinians' appearance elicited a lethal volley from the 73rd Ohio. Lt. Col. William H. Wallace of the 18th South Carolina reported, "Here some of our best officers fell, among them Colonel Gadberry. He fell pierced by a ball through the heart and expired almost immediately." In spite of Gadberry's death, the 18th South Carolina stood its ground and "vigorously returned" fire at the 73rd Ohio. Evans's South Carolinians were giving McLean's left wing all it could handle.[23]

Farther to the right, the resurgent 5th Texas with some hearty members of the Holcombe Legion emerged from the woods on the right flank of the 18th South Carolina. The Texans overlapped McLean's left flank and opened a vicious enfilading fire into the 73rd Ohio. The Buckeyes reflexively refused their left flank and continued to resist the Texans. The Southerners still outflanked the Federals, and the Ohioans fell in droves. When at almost the same time Colonel Corse's brigade appeared in the distance, the Buckeyes' battle line shuddered.

There was nothing for the 73rd Ohio to do but retreat under a deadly crossfire of musketry and artillery. Seeing the Federals faltering, the Texans and South Carolinians bolted out of the woods and chased after the Ohioans, firing as they went. A platoon of Buckeyes sought shelter behind a garden fence, but the Southerners quickly overran the position and captured the beaten Federals. As the Ohioans retreated toward Chinn Branch, Rebel bullets cut down their color bearer, leaving the 73rd Ohio's battle flag lying on the ground. With the Confederates nearly upon the stricken colors, Capt. John Madeira of the 73rd Ohio sprinted back in the midst of the fire, seized the colors, and returned to his regiment. The overwhelmed Buckeyes streamed past the Chinn House under a galling fire, crossed Chinn Branch, and rallied behind a fence in the woods between Chinn Branch and Sudley Road.[24]

With Rebel bullets zipping through the air, Colonel McLean saw the 73rd Ohio disintegrate and ordered the balance of his brigade to change front to the left in order to meet the gray tide. Col. William Richardson of the 25th Ohio attempted to execute the maneuver, but "the fire was so terrible and the noise of battle so great that it was impossible to be heard or do anything without confusion." Seeing the colors of the 73rd Ohio falling to the ground and Rebels rushing to capture them, the 25th Ohio broke. Caught in the same vise that flattened the 73rd Ohio, the 25th Ohio streamed over the crest of Chinn Ridge and retreated toward the woods in their rear. As McLean's left wing gave way, Captain Wiedrich's gunners followed suit and retired to Henry Hill.[25]

While McLean's men were battling on Chinn Ridge, McDowell had dispatched reinforcements to the beleaguered Union left, personally leading Brig. Gen. Zealous Bates Tower's command of two brigades and two batteries from Brig. Gen. James Ricketts's division to Henry Hill. McDowell's actions impressed those who saw him. One soldier noted that the troops had never witnessed McDowell "so vigorously bold and aggressive or the lines of his face deepen with such intense anxiety." He seemed to be the personification of heroism, as he led Tower's troops southward down the Sudley Road "amid the bursting of rebel shells." The column crossed the Warrenton Turnpike and ascended the northern slope of Henry Hill, passing many wounded men from Porter's command lying on the side of the road. Although unable to move, the stricken Northerners shouted, "Pitch in boys and give 'em hell."[26]

McDowell had temporarily halted Tower's men on Henry Hill, where he encountered a courier from Pope. He, who had all along ignored the overwhelming evidence of the threat to his left, asked McDowell via a staff officer if he "had not taken too much from the right." Inconceivably, Pope still failed to grasp the magnitude of this Confederate threat. McDowell, however, understood the severity of the Confederate attack and explained it to Pope when he arrived on Henry Hill a few minutes later. Pope "sanctioned" McDowell's actions, and Tower marched toward Chinn Ridge.[27]

Brigadier General Tower was born in Massachusetts in 1819. He had graduated from West Point, ranked first in the class of 1841. Serving on Gen. Winfield Scott's staff during the Mexican War, Tower won several brevets for gallantry. Although relatively new to his infantry command, he quickly gained a reputation as a strict disciplinarian who was "not very popular with the boys." Nevertheless, he earned the respect of his men. A soldier of the 26th New York wrote that "a better or braver [officer] does not exist." On August 30 the Bay Stater commanded a demi-division composed of his own brigade and that of Brig. Gen. George L. Hartsuff, the latter being absent because of illness. Although Col. John W. Stiles of the 83rd New York officially commanded Hartsuff's brigade, Tower called the shots on Chinn Ridge.[28]

Tower galloped ahead of his command and found McLean's Ohioans and Wiedrich's New Yorkers fronting westward and battling the Texans and South Carolinians of Evans's command. Leaving Hartsuff's brigade on Henry Hill's western slope between Chinn Branch and Sudley Road, Tower double-quicked his own brigade into position, but the hurried pace scattered and disoriented his command. One Federal complained, "If we had been taken in on common time, our ranks would not have been broken."[29]

The situation did not look promising to Tower's men, even before they began fighting. "The men were much fatigued however and completely worn out. Many had no shoes and all were tired and weary from loss of sleep and rest for many days in succession. To sum it up, we were in no condition to fight a great battle."[30] Nevertheless, Tower's men mustered the courage and physical strength to answer the call of duty.

The same tempest that unhinged McLean's left wing welcomed Tower's brigade to Chinn Ridge, forcing it to deploy under fire. The 2nd Maine Battery unlimbered on Bald Hill, two hundred yards behind Tower's left flank, and fired into Kemper's mass of Confederates approaching from the south, inhibiting their ability to regroup and advance along Chinn Branch. Col. William H. Christian's 26th New York formed its line of battle on Tower's left flank, behind Cooper's battery. Lt. Col. Joseph McLean's 88th Pennsylvania followed the New Yorkers, occupying the center of the brigade's battle line. Col. Peter Lyle's 90th Pennsylvania filed into position on the 88th Regiment's right flank and lay flat on the ground to avoid the projectiles overshooting the Ohioans on the front line. Capt. George F. Leppien's 5th Maine Light Battery and Col. Adrian Root's 94th New York brought up the rear of Tower's column and were still moving into position on Chinn Ridge when Tower's left came under fire.[31] John D. Vautier of the 88th Pennsylvania recalled the deployment of Tower's brigade:

> The confusion among the troops on the hill was great; officers and men shouting, shells tearing through and exploding, the incessant rattle of the muskets, the cries of the wounded, all combined made up a scene that was anything but encouraging, yet every one appeared anxious to get in the proper place to do the most good.[32]

Seeing the pressure building against McLean's brigade, Tower ordered Colonel Christian to quickly advance the 26th New York into a position on the left flank of the 73rd Ohio. Its soldiers were already breaking for the rear under the slicing flank fire from the Texans. Only the two left-flank companies of the 26th New York successfully carried out their orders and extended the Ohioans' line to the left. These New Yorkers quickly spotted the approaching Texans in their front and opened fire. The remaining eight companies of the 26th New York remained idle, the Ohioans masking their firing lanes. As the New Yorkers moved toward the crest of Chinn Ridge, Cooper's Pennsylvania gunners rammed home their last rounds of ammunition, fired a final blast into the approaching Confederates, limbered their guns, and narrowly escaped, the Texans capturing two caissons that were left behind. Both the battery and panic-stricken Ohioans crashed through the advancing 26th New York, carrying it into the valley of Chinn Branch. The confusion on Chinn Ridge also alarmed the gunners of the 2nd Maine Battery on Bald Hill, causing them to withdraw.[33]

The Pennsylvania gunners dashed away from Chinn Ridge with the Texans in hot pursuit, and barely escaped them. A team of "four large white or gray horses" driven by one artillerist raced down Chinn Ridge at a "sweeping gallop," racing past Eppa Hunton's Virginians in the valley. The Virginians fired a volley at the fleeing Union gunner, but he had luck on his side, and the Confederates missed their mark. As he dashed past Hunton's line, an officer shouted, "Let the man alone and shoot at the horses!" The brave artillerist kept moving and eventually escaped. As he passed over a hill to safety, he took off his cap and "waved it around his head several times," evoking cheers from many of Hunton's Virginians.[34]

Capt. H. T. Owen of the 18th Virginia later pondered the artillerist's fate: "I suppose at least five hundred men fired at that Yankee when he passed the head of the ditch. Our men were within seventy-five yards of him. I have often wondered if he escaped death in other battles and whether he now lives to tell of the fearful gauntlet he ran along the front of a whole brigade of Rebels firing at him."[35]

In Tower's center, Wiedrich's battery had retreated through the ranks of the 88th Pennsylvania, but the Keystone State men withstood the onslaught of fugitive soldiers, horses, and cannon, and held their ground. On Tower's right flank, the 90th Pennsylvania had barely hit the ground when McDowell ordered Colonel Lyle to move to the crest of the ridge. If McDowell still held any hopes of stopping the Confederates at Chinn Ridge, they sank rapidly with the retreat of McLean's left wing.[36]

The situation had attained crisis proportions for the Army of Virginia. If the 5th Texas, Evans, and Corse could seize Chinn Ridge, the balance of Kemper's division could immediately drive on to Henry Hill, closely supported by Brig. Gen. David R. Jones's division; Longstreet could achieve his objective. It was of the utmost urgency that the Federals hold Chinn Ridge until Pope secured Henry Hill with other troops. Tower's men were attempting to engage the Southerners, but because they were caught up in the chaos and confusion caused by the retreating Ohioans and artillerists, they could offer no immediate assistance. For the next few minutes, the fate of the Union army at Manassas depended on McLean's two remaining regiments, the 55th and 75th Ohio. If they failed, the Confederates could quickly sweep Tower off the ridge before he could effectively employ his troops, and Chinn Ridge would be lost—and with it perhaps much of Pope's army.

Four

"We Went for Them"

When Nathaniel McLean ordered the change of front, the 75th Ohio attempted a left wheel, but Wiedrich's retreating guns crashed through its line. The 75th Ohio then "doubled up like a hinge so that the right and left companies came together." As a result, only companies A and B of the 75th successfully changed front. Seeing the 75th Ohio waver, Col. John C. Lee called out to the 55th Ohio, "Stand to it boys, and do not run!" Under a heavy crossfire, the 55th Ohio wheeled to the left and advanced toward the emboldened South Carolinians and Texans. As the Ohioans turned to face their enemy, Colonel Lee noticed that his regimental flag was concealed in its casing and bellowed out, "Unfurl and let them see that flag!" The 55th's color bearer "dashed it out upon the air" in a scene of martial grandeur, which inspirited the soldiers from Northern Ohio. Advancing proudly beneath their royal blue banner adorned with a large bald eagle, the 55th Ohio marched into one of the war's deadliest maelstroms. As one Buckeye put it, "We went for them."[1]

With fixed bayonets, the 55th Ohio and two companies of the 75th Ohio fired several destructive volleys into the left flank of the 17th South Carolina. The 17th broke for the woods, exposing the left flank of the 18th South Carolina, which quickly followed suit. The South Carolinians fled through the Chinn orchard "like the devil was after them," according to one Buckeye. When Pvt. D. H. Gilliland of the 55th Ohio saw the Confederates in headlong flight, he jumped up in the air and shouted, "Give it to them boys, we have them a-going now!" Nathaniel McLean proudly recalled, "My men obeyed my orders in this great extremity under a heavy fire in grand style, delivering their fire . . . so steadily and with such terrible effect that the advance of the enemy was checked at once."[2]

Closer to the Chinn House, the 5th Texas likewise trembled under the shock of the Ohioans' attack. A Yankee bullet struck Colonel Robertson as he passed through the garden gate, depriving the Texans of their leader. Under the leaden storm, the Texans scattered throughout the Chinn yard. Some sheltered themselves behind the house and outbuildings, most in a wash on the southeast face of Chinn Ridge. Without help, the 5th Texas was going nowhere.[3]

While the Southerners sought cover, McLean rallied remnants of the 25th, 73rd, and 75th Ohio, placing them on the 55th Ohio's left flank. For a few seconds, there was a lull on Chinn Ridge. The 55th Ohio had temporarily stalled the Confederate momentum there but had no time to rest; Corse's brigade of Kemper's division was rapidly approaching the Chinn House.[4]

Col. Montgomery Corse, a banker from Alexandria, Virginia, had attended military school and commanded a company of Virginians in the Mexican War. When the Civil War broke out, Corse joined the 17th Virginia Infantry and ably led it at First Manassas, Williamsburg, Seven Pines, and Frayser's Farm. His former commander, Maj. Gen. Ambrose P. Hill, praised Corse as "calm and equable as a May morn, more himself like a true soldier throughout." His quiet, gentle demeanor earned him the epithet "Grandmother Corse." His brigade had suffered heavy casualties on the Peninsula and understood the brutal reality of war.[5]

His brigade had steeled itself for action in the fields of the William Lewis Farm. When the time to move arrived, Lt. Col. Morton Marye of the 17th Virginia called out, "Fall in now men, steady lads—steady Seventeenth." The men stripped for the fight and deposited their "superfluous equipment" into a large pile, leaving guards to watch over it. Pvt. Alexander Hunter looked around and noted, "The time for action had come. . . . The stern compres-

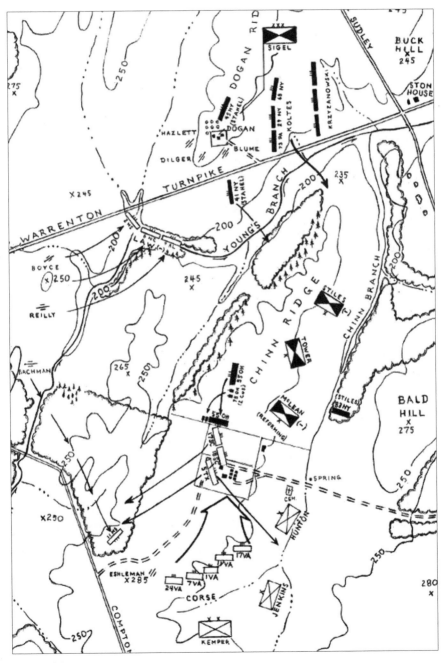

John C. McAnaw

sion of the lip, and determined flash of the eye, as they tightened the belt of their cartridge boxes, spoke louder words that their minds were made up—to do—or to die."[6]

In Kemper's advance toward the Chinn House, Corse's brigade had followed 250 yards behind Hunton's. When Hunton failed to make his change of front, the opportunity to rout the Ohioans landed in Corse's lap. Corse quickly swung his right flank around and aimed it toward the Chinn House. As the Virginians advanced, Evans's South Carolinians and Texans retreated past Corse's men in "utter rout and confusion." Some of the terror-stricken Southerners shouted to the 1st Virginia, "Go back!" Others cried out, "Lie down!" while the more resolute urged a rapid advance.[7]

On Corse's right flank, the 17th Virginia led the way. Its commander, Lieutenant Colonel Marye, "dismounted, drew his sword from the scabbard, and looking the beau ideal of a soldier, placed himself at the head of his men." The 17th Virginia passed by the eastern side of the Chinn House and attacked the remnants of the 25th, 73rd, and 75th Ohio crouching behind a stone wall. The 88th and 90th Pennsylvania of Tower's brigade changed front and came up behind the Ohioans' left, which prevented the 90th Pennsylvania's right wing from firing. The Buckeyes and Pennsylvanians fired "a withering volley at point-blank pistol range" that struck the Virginians "with the fury of a thunderbolt."

As the 17th Virginia wavered, Marye shouted, "Steady men—keep cool boys—Steady!" Hearing Marye's familiar, reassuring voice, the Virginians re-formed their line and fired back at the Federals. But when a bullet "frightfully shattered" Marye's knee, the battle line of the 17th Virginia broke. The situation was no different in the 1st and 11th Virginia on Marye's left. Confusion reigned, as the Virginians fell killed or wounded under the blistering rifle fire. Nevertheless, these veteran Virginia fighters rose to the urgency of the situation.[8] The 17th Virginia's Pvt. Alexander Hunter recalled,

> Now individual bravery made up for the disaster. The officers surged ahead with their swords waving in the air, cheering on the men, who kept close to their heels, loading and firing as they ran. The line of blue

CORSE ATTACKS

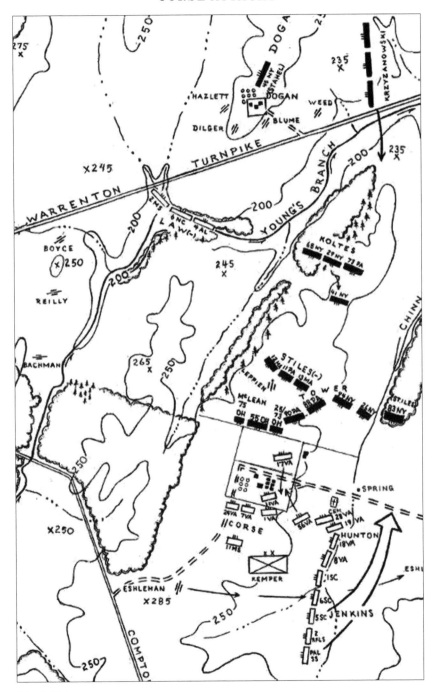

John C. McAnaw

was not fifty yards distant and every man took a sure, close aim before his finger pressed the trigger. It was a decisive fight of about ten minutes, both sides stood gamely to their work.[9]

On the west side of the Chinn House, Col. William Tazewell Patton's 7th Virginia found the Chinn House and outbuildings blocking its advance. A great-uncle of Gen. George S. Patton of World War II fame, Patton marched his regiment by the left oblique and passed around the obstructions. Several Texans firing from the southwest corner of the Chinn House heard shouts of "forward" and joined the 7th Virginia as it passed. When the Virginians and Texans closed to within forty yards of the Ohioans, the 55th Ohio rose up and fired a volley at the Southerners that "cut them all to pieces," according to Ohio Pvt. John W. Rumpel. Unable to withstand the musketry, the Virginians and Texans "turned and fled like dogs," lamented Pvt. Robert Campbell of the 5th Texas. Three color bearers from the 7th Virginia fell in rapid succession. Lt. Frederick Boalt of the 55th Ohio saw an opportunity and shouted, "Let's have those colors!" Boalt and a few other Buckeyes raced toward the "hated" flag, but before the Federals could claim their prize, twenty-one-year-old Lt. Col. Charles C. Floweree snatched the flag up and carried it back to the Confederate battle line where he waved it overhead, rallying the staggered 7th Virginia. Moments later, a Yankee bullet severely wounded Patton, leaving the youthful Floweree in command of the 7th Virginia.[10]

On Corse's left flank, the Chinn outbuildings also blocked the advance of the 24th Virginia, which came up behind the 7th Virginia. This outfit transformed its battle line into a marching column to maneuver around the buildings, a difficult exercise in the face of enemy fire. Col. William R. Terry, a graduate of the Virginia Military Institute, worked feverishly to move the 24th Virginia past the Chinn House as the Union troops showered it with bullets. Lt. Col. Peter Hairston fell wounded, and the 24th Virginia became entangled with the retreating 7th Virginia in its attempt to avoid the buildings. Nevertheless, Terry kept the men from breaking and persisted in his efforts while the rest of the brigade engaged McLean's Ohioans. Colonel Stevens joined Terry with some of his South Carolinians and assisted him in rallying the Virginians, but it would take more time to regroup their jumbled ranks.[11]

Meanwhile, in the valley of Chinn Branch, Eppa Hunton reformed his troops and ordered a change of front to join the fight on the ridge. In doing so, Hunton redirected his advance away from Longstreet's strategic objective—Henry Hill. Since his inexperienced division commander, James Kemper, did not provide such guidance to his brigadiers, Hunton did what came naturally to the aggressive Virginian: attack the nearest Federals. Hunton placed himself at the head of his lead regiment, the 56th Virginia, followed by the 28th, 19th, and 18th Virginia. The 8th Virginia on Hunton's right flank did not follow but remained fronted east with Jenkins's brigade. Marching in column, his Virginians filed to the left and headed back toward Chinn Ridge. As Hunton's men started up the slope, the 88th Pennsylvania rose up and poured a "most destructive" fire into the Virginians. Stunned by the volley, Col. Robert C. Allen halted the 28th Virginia, the second regiment in Hunton's column, blocking the advance of the brigade's remaining regiments. Hunton did not realize what had occurred and moved on with the 56th Virginia, which came up behind the 17th Virginia on Corse's left flank, while the Pennsylvanians pummeled the two stalled regiments.[12]

Once Hunton's Virginians began moving, they encountered fierce resistance from the 88th Pennsylvania of Tower's brigade. "Grape, shell and minié balls raked our line from one end to the other," recalled Capt. Richard Irby of the 18th Virginia. Tower's fierce resistance exacted a heavy toll on the Confederate ranks. The 19th and 28th Virginia incurred 70 percent of the casualties suffered by Hunton's brigade, with 152 men killed and wounded. A Pennsylvania soldier proudly proclaimed that Tower's men "almost annihilated" the Southerners, who fell back to Chinn Branch. Yet there would be no rest for Tower's men; Gen. Micah Jenkins's South Carolina brigade would soon be entering the battle.[13]

Zealous Tower responded to this new threat by shifting Col. Adrian Root's 94th New York from his right to his left flank. By the time the New Yorkers reached the left flank, the 88th was already engaged with Hunton's Virginians and blocked the 94th New York from firing. The New Yorkers filed farther east down the slope of the ridge into the valley of Chinn Branch, where they joined a reformed battalion from the 26th New York. The limited space permitted Root to deploy only seven of his ten companies, so Tower rushed the remaining three back to his right flank. The troops in the valley had no time for preparations; the Southerners were already advancing.

On Kemper's right flank, Jenkins belatedly realized that his South Carolinians had bypassed the combat on Chinn Ridge. Most of his brigade had already crossed to the east bank of Chinn Branch. Jenkins followed Hunton's lead and turned away from the lightly defended Henry Hill to join the fighting on Chinn Ridge. Jenkins dashed over to Col. Thomas J. Glover, commander of the 1st South Carolina Volunteers, on the brigade's left flank, ordering him to "change front and begin the attack." Jenkins assured Glover that he would support him as soon as he could. For now, only the left wing of the 6th South Carolina followed Glover's regiment toward Chinn Ridge. As the South Carolinians changed front toward the combat, they ran into the 8th Virginia of Hunton's brigade, which had not yet changed its direction. The 8th's Lt. Col. Norborne Berkeley saw the South Carolinians approaching and reacted accordingly, changing his front and advancing on the left flank of the 1st South Carolina. As the South Carolinians and Virginians moved forward, the 5th Texas leaped out of its sheltering wash and joined the advance on the left flank of the 8th Virginia.

Before the 1st and 6th South Carolina, 8th Virginia, and 5th Texas advanced, Tower's Federals had been directing their fire at Hunton's Virginians. The appearance of these additional Confederates diluted the firepower of Tower's Pennsylvanians, who now had to redirect much of their musketry. This allowed the officers of Hunton's faltering Virginia regiments to steady their men and maintain their positions. Amid the chaos, Col. James B. Strange of the 19th Virginia stepped forward and renewed the attack. Upon Strange's order, the 18th, 19th, and 28th Virginia regiments moved into position to the right of Corse's 17th Virginia.

The opportunity to rally Hunton's men came at the expense of the 1st South Carolina and 5th Texas. The Federal fire cut down several of their officers and many of their enlisted men. In the words of the 1st South Carolina's

Col. James R. Hagood, "confusion and disorder followed" the Federal blast. One Texan painfully reported, "Terrific volleys, perfect storms of bullets were poured into our bleeding ranks, until it seemed impossible for a man to live a moment in such a storm of death." Still, the South Carolinians, Texans, and Virginians held their ground and shot back at the Federals amid this leaden hail. Tower's Federals fell in droves, weakening the amount of fire the Federals could apply to the ever-increasing numbers of Confederates. The Confederate fire, fretted one Federal, "came from so many directions that our men were at a loss how to return it effectively." Meanwhile, Jenkins's remaining regiments advanced east of Chinn Branch toward Bald Hill.[14]

Maj. Gen. Irvin McDowell spotted Jenkins's right wing advancing down the east bank of Chinn Branch. He rushed over to Stiles's idle troops on the western slope of Henry Hill, "cursing like a pirate and wanting to know who gave orders to place the brigade there." McDowell first sent three regiments to Chinn Ridge and detached the 83rd New York into the woods on Bald Hill, east of Chinn Branch, to confront Jenkins's right wing. The troops who went to Chinn Ridge marveled at how "entire regiments seemed to melt away" under the Confederate musketry. On Bald Hill, Maj. Allen Rutherford positioned the 83rd New York, ordering the men to kneel on one knee behind a rail fence at the wood line. Col. Orland Smith rallied a hundred men from the 73rd Ohio and joined the New Yorkers at the fence line. Another battalion from the 26th New York and other units also rallied, adding their firepower to this patchwork battle line. When the first wave of Jenkins's right wing neared the wood line, the New Yorkers and Ohioans fired into the South Carolinians, who "went down like ripe grain." Unable to make any headway, Jenkins's men fell back behind a rise and waited for their comrades. From Chinn Ridge to Bald Hill, the outgunned Union troops desperately resisted the massive Confederate assault. A soldier of the 83rd New York recalled in awe how Chinn Ridge "blazed with fire, [and] its foundation shook with the roar of the guns."[15]

On top of the ridge, Lt. W. F. Twitchell led Capt. George Leppien's 5th Maine Battery into position on Tower's right. As the Maine men dashed up the ridge, they passed through the greatly reduced ranks of the 88th

Pennsylvania, throwing it into much disorder. The 90th Pennsylvania's Col. Peter Lyle received advance notice of the deploying battery and withdrew from the firing line. When guns were arrayed, they opened fire, and Colonel Lyle posted the remnants of the 90th Pennsylvania back on Leppien's right. Ironically, the confusion created by the deployment of this fresh battery significantly reduced the volume of rifle fire that the Federal infantry had been pouring into the Confederates.[16]

Tower's regimental officers exerted themselves to hold the battle line. Prominent among them was Lt. Col. Joseph A. McLean (no relation to Nathaniel McLean), also known as Colonel Joe to the men of the 88th Pennsylvania. Eight days earlier, McLean had confided to his wife, "Kiss my dear little ones for me and assure yourself I will do all I can to save myself *consistent with honor.* I feel first rate my trust is in God! But at the same time, I want to keep my powder dry."[17]

When the 88th Pennsylvania faltered, Colonel Joe rode among his men, rallying them on the colors. As he did, a Confederate bullet struck his thigh, rupturing the femoral artery and knocking him from his horse. The stirrup entangled McLean's foot, and the horse ran off, dragging the wounded Pennsylvanian along. Lt. William J. Rannells of the 75th Ohio caught the horse and freed McLean's leg from the stirrup. The Ohioan then applied a leather tourniquet and stemmed the flow of blood. Rannells and three men of the 88th Pennsylvania attempted to carry McLean to a hospital, but Colonel Joe saw the Confederates closing in and cried out, "Boys, drop me and save yourselves for I must die." The three Pennsylvanians dropped McLean without warning, knocking his tourniquet loose. Rannells tightened the leather strap and remained with McLean as the Confederates surged by.

As McLean lay there, another bullet struck him in the calf. Lieutenant Rannells sought aid from approaching Confederates, but they demurred and ordered him to the rear as a prisoner of war. As Rannells departed, McLean called out, "Tell my wife she will never blush to be my widow. I die for my Country and the old flag." Later, Lieutenant Rannells penned a letter to McLean's wife telling of his death, which Rannells sent to his sister, Cora. She in turn passed the sad news to McLean's family and friends in Pennsylvania.[18]

While the Confederate infantry attacked the Federals on Chinn Ridge, the Southern artillery made its presence felt from several directions. Capt. W. K. Bachman's German Artillery from South Carolina and a section of the Dixie Artillery received the assignment and moved under a shower of shells from the powerful Federal batteries on Dogan Ridge. Bachman described his battery's advance:

> I went onto a field where the Texas brigade and Hampton Legion engaged the Zouaves. The ground was covered with the dead red-breeched fellows so that I had actually to pilot the drivers through the bodies, sometimes stopping to move them out of the way. The wounded Zouaves and our men lay near each other; some of my men gave them water, and in return, they gave them their red caps, etc.[19]

Not all of the batteries showed the same care and compassion displayed by Bachman. One Confederate later recalled, "I saw there where the army wagons or artillery had run over the dead Yankees, crushing them into the ground, which was a horrible sight to behold. It was inhuman, could have been avoided. No man with a conscience would have done such a thing."[20]

Although a Federal shell disabled one of Bachman's guns, he deployed his remaining pieces atop the hill overlooking Young's Branch. A section of the Dixie Artillery unlimbered and went into action nearby. From there, the Southern gunners focused their attention on the Federal batteries atop Chinn Ridge. Their shells created havoc among the Federal infantry supporting Leppien's battery. To the south, Colonel Rosser brilliantly maneuvered his three batteries to key positions. A Georgian of Brig. Gen. David R. Jones's division penned this praise:

> For the first time, I saw artillery charge. Two pieces would be driven at a gallop to a knoll, unlimber and fire, while two others would gallop past them to another eminence, and commence firing, when the first couple would, like trained dogs, rush past them to get position. Thus alternating, this artillery was kept ahead of us and actually drove

the enemy some distance before we could overtake them although we were in a run.[21]

The artillery fire added more smoke to the scene of Chinn Ridge and demoralized the already dazed Federals.

Farther west on the ridge, Brig. Gen. Robert Schenck, McLean's divisional commander, saw McLean's numbers dwindling as the Ohioans grudgingly gave ground. Schenck looked around and spotted the 12th Massachusetts standing idly on the reverse slope of Chinn Ridge. Schenck galloped up to them and shouted, "Who is in command here?" They replied, "We don't know. Our general is gone." Schenck looked around and inquired, "What regiment is that?" An officer proudly chimed, "The Twelfth Massachusetts." "Good," replied Schenck. "Tell the officer in command to form on the right of that [McLean's] brigade." While Schenck bolstered the right flank, McDowell rode up to the 13th Massachusetts and shifted it to the left. There, the Bay Staters joined the 94th New York in keeping the Southerners away from Tower's left flank.[22]

Col. Fletcher Webster guided the 12th Massachusetts into position on the 55th Ohio's right flank. Webster was the eldest and only surviving child of the noted orator and defender of the Union, Senator Daniel Webster. On the morning of the battle, Colonel Webster wrote his wife, "This may be my last letter, dear love; for I shall not spare myself—God bless and protect you and the dear, darling children. We are all under his protection." The Bay Staters went into their first battle with some trepidation, but the firing of their first volley chased their fears away. Now they stood coolly, loading and firing into the 24th Virginia.[23]

The fields west of the Chinn House flamed with musketry. The combatants blazed away at one another with unabated fury for ten bloody minutes. Remnants of Evans's brigade fired into the Federals from the woods on the right flank. As the Southern musketry increased, Colonel Lee shouted to the 55th Ohio, "Stand to it, boys. Stand your ground." The regiment had not lost many men until now, "when they began to fall pretty fast." The 55th Ohio did not break, but as the pressure grew, the men instinctively drew back, taking a few steps rearward with each successive shot. They faced toward their enemy but were being driven slowly and inexorably rearward.[24]

As the fighting raged, General Schenck brought up the 11th Pennsylvania to bolster the sagging battle line. He called out to McLean, "Where will you have them?" "On my left flank," shouted McLean. Then Schenck, the Ohioans' "Old Bulldog," dashed back to the 55th Ohio and shouted, "Boys, give the rebels hell." He brandished his sword and whirled it overhead as he rode along the ragged battle line and cheered McLean's remaining men. Suddenly, a bullet shot off one of Schenck's fingertips; another struck him in the side but glanced off his sword belt, leaving only a contusion. A third missile shattered his right forearm and sent his sword sailing through the air. A staff officer grabbed the reins of Schenck's horse and assisted him from the saddle. His staff officers attempted to carry him to safety, but he refused to leave without his sword. Someone finally retrieved it, and the staff officers and orderlies carried the severely wounded Schenck to the rear, he having fought his last battle.[25]

Despite the heroic resistance by the Union soldiers, Confederate numbers and bravery began to tell. The Confederate attack received an unexpected boost when Col. Phillip F. Liddell's 11th Mississippi strayed from Col. Evander Law's brigade along the Warrenton Turnpike. As the Mississippians marched to the sound of intense gunfire, one of them was reminded of "canebrake on fire." The Mississippians joined the fight on Corse's left in the Chinn orchard and raked the 12th Massachusetts right flank with gunfire. Webster urged his men to stand firm, but a Confederate bullet cut him down. It ripped through his arm and entered his body, slamming him from his horse into the ground.[26]

Three comrades attempted to carry Webster to safety, but the Confederates shot one of the bearers, prompting another to run off. The last one, his adjutant, pulled Webster under some brush in a little hollow; the two men remained out of sight, though caught between two battle lines and taking fire from both friend and foe. Webster told his adjutant to save himself, but the faithful aide remained at Webster's side. The first Confederates who overran Webster's position refused to carry him away and ordered his aide to the rear as a prisoner. He refused to abandon Webster, so the Southerners forced him to the rear at bayonet point. It mattered little; the last of Daniel Webster's children would be dead within the hour.[27]

Not all of the Southerners lacked compassion. Pvt. Ludwell Hutchison of the 8th Virginia had approached the fallen Bay State officer and attempted to comfort him. Webster asked Hutchison to send his wallet to his family. Hutchison promised to do so, and when the war ended, he returned the wallet. Webster gave his ring to another soldier from the 19th Virginia who later died at Antietam. Nevertheless, the ring eventually made its way back to Mrs. Webster, thanks to the efforts of another Virginian.

On McLean's opposite flank, the 11th Pennsylvania battled the 11th and 17th Virginia of Corse's brigade. One Keystone State man remembered, "Instantly our fire opened and in as many minutes our flag went down five times." As the 11th went into position, a Confederate bullet snuffed out the life of Lt. Col. Thomas S. Martin. Another mortally wounded Maj. Henry A. Frink. Enlisted men fell by the dozen. A Minié ball struck Col. Richard Coulter's horse in the neck, but the colonel escaped unharmed. In a matter of minutes, the 11th Pennsylvania lost 105 men killed or wounded, while another 86 came up missing, many of them dead on the field before the battle ended.[28]

From the 11th Mississippi on Kemper's left flank to Jenkins's Carolinians near Chinn Branch, the Southerners overlapped both flanks of the Federal position on Chinn Ridge. Lt. William N. Wood of the 19th Virginia noted, "The hill was gallantly defended, and it was only when the impetuous, yelling, dashing Confederates had nearly surrounded the hill that the enemy broke and fled." Colonel Terry advanced the 24th Virginia on Corse's left flank, accompanied by remnants of Evans's brigade. The 24th Virginia "delivered a destructive volley" into the 12th Massachusetts and 55th Ohio. With youthful exuberance, Lieutenant Colonel Floweree rallied the 7th Virginia and shouted, "Up to the fence, 7th Regiment, and give them hell!" His men in turn bolted to the barrier and laced the Federals with a volley. On Corse's right flank, the 17th Virginia let out a "wild yell" and rushed the beaten Federals. Pvt. Sam Coleman sprinted ahead of the pack and grabbed the

11th Pennsylvania's national colors from the hands of the wounded color sergeant.[29]

As Corse's Virginians advanced, Lieutenant Twitchell's Maine gunners roared into action and fired at the 24th Virginia, briefly checking the approaching Confederates. The Virginians responded with a deadly volley, slaughtering most of Leppien's horses in their traces. The surviving mounts ran off with the caissons, leaving the gunners little ammunition to continue the fight. At the same time, their infantry support dissipated as the Southerners closed in. Col. Frederick Skinner of the 1st Virginia Infantry stood up in his stirrups and bellowed, "Forward, old First—Follow me!" Skinner spurred his horse and bolted into the midst of Leppien's battery, whirled his sword through the air, and cut down a Federal who was about to pull the lanyard. Another Federal reached for the lanyard and met the same fate. The Maine gunners "fought like Tigers" as dozens of Virginians swarmed over the guns. The Federal infantry fired into the teeming Confederates around the guns, striking Skinner with three balls. Skinner reeled and headed to the rear severely wounded. Seeing one of his men, he called out, "Jack, bear me witness that I was the first man on that battery." Pvt. John "Jack" Dooley replied, "I will, Colonel," as he bandaged Skinner's severely wounded forearm.[30]

Seeing Confederates among Leppien's guns, Col. John C. Lee ordered the 55th Ohio to retreat as the Federal line collapsed. Capt. Charles Gambee reasoned, "The 55th fought nobly, but was obliged to give way before vastly superior numbers." One Buckeye stayed on the ridge long enough to fire three rounds after the regiment departed. When he looked to his left, he saw Confederates turning Leppien's guns on his retreating comrades and knew it was time to go.[31]

McLean had sat on his horse and watched the remnants of his brigade stream past him. Before leaving the ridge, McLean turned and took one last look at the enemy when a Union battle flag fluttering in the breeze caught his attention. McLean looked again and realized that the flag's wounded bearer was sitting upright supporting the colors of the 75th Ohio. Michael Brady, an eighteen-year-old Irish lad, had carried the colors that McLean saw into battle at Manassas for the first time. Back in May at the battle of Mc-

Dowell, the 75th Ohio had fought sheltered behind the crest of a steep hill. During the engagement, the Confederates shot the regiment's color bearer, and the flag tumbled down the hill toward the Confederates. Only five feet four, Brady leaped over the crest of the hill, snatched the flag, and flaunted it at the Confederates. For his bravery, the men of the 75th Ohio demanded that Brady be appointed color bearer. McLean held up the appointment for several weeks, believing Brady too small for the job. Finally, McLean relented and officially named Brady the 75th Ohio's color bearer.

On this day at Manassas, Lt. George B. Fox had jokingly called to Brady, "They will get the colors today," when the Southerners first appeared. Brady turned to look at the Confederates issuing forth from the woods and loudly declared, "If they get the flag, they'll get old Mike. Now mind that, Lieutenant." As the Confederates enveloped McLean's final position, Brady rushed forward and waved the flag "back and forth in a defiant manner," hoping to rally the troops. A Confederate bullet soon shattered the flagstaff, and another pierced the gallant Brady's body. He fell to the ground, but quickly sat up and held the flag aloft. Seeing their regimental flag, McLean, Capt. Andrew Harris, and a few men ran back to retrieve the colors. Although mortally wounded, Brady refused to release his grip. Harris pried each finger off the staff to free it from Brady's devoted grasp.[32]

McLean's brigade—rather the 55th and 75th Ohio—retreated along the western slope of Chinn Ridge. The intervening crest screened the Ohioans from Kemper's powerful right flank, while Tower's men suffered immensely on the opposite side of the crest. McLean turned to his adjutant and complained, "We had been sent up there and sacrificed." McLean later recalled, "I do not know that I was ever so angry . . . in all my life." His adjutant tried to calm McLean, but he continued, declaring, "It's the literal truth." As the 55th Ohio slowly retreated through the pastures of Hazel Plain, the Confederate artillery wreaked havoc in the blue ranks. Sgt. Luther B. Mesnard recalled, "As I fell in on the right, I saw color bearer [William] Bellamy's head strike the ground some twenty feet in rear of the line, while his body with the colors fell forward, a solid shot having struck him in the chin." The Ohioans continued their retreat down the slope of Chinn Ridge and crossed Young's

Branch. Once across, McLean's men followed the Warrenton Turnpike east toward the Stone House.[33]

To the right of Leppien's guns, Colonel Lyle's 90th Pennsylvania held its position too long and paid the price for its bravery. Before the Pennsylvanians realized it, more Confederates had overrun the battery. Although their position just west of the ridge's crest had saved the Pennsylvanians from suffering heavy losses in killed and wounded, it had also concealed the proximity of the Confederates on their left. As a result, the Confederates scooped up 162 prisoners from the 90th Pennsylvania before it could withdraw.

While the Federal line fell apart on Chinn Ridge, Capt. Robert M. Stribling's Fauquier Artillery advanced to a commanding eminence near Jenkins's right flank between Chinn Branch and Sudley Road. Stribling's Virginians opened fire and pelted the 26th and 83rd New York and the 73rd Ohio with case shot and canister. The right wing of Jenkins's South Carolina brigade renewed its advance, backed by Col. Henry L. Benning's brigade of Georgians. Before this imposing Confederate force struck, Major Rutherford led the 83rd New York through the woods toward Sudley Road. The Carolinians now opened fire on the remaining Federals who hastily abandoned their position. But the Ohioans and New Yorkers did not go easily. As they withdrew, they sometimes halted, turned, and fired at the approaching Confederates before continuing the retreat. Nevertheless, the withdrawal of these Federals from the timber on the fringe of Bald Hill exposed Tower's left flank east of Chinn Branch.

On Tower's extreme left flank, the 13th Massachusetts and 94th New York struggled with the 1st South Carolina, 5th Texas, and 8th Virginia. One Carolinian declared, "Officers and men became mad with excitement, and like an infuriated mob, yelling and firing, they charged the enemy." The Federal line quivered under the renewed assault, and Tower rode out in front of the shaken New Englanders and New Yorkers. When the Southerners closed to within twenty-five yards, Tower shouted to the 13th Massachusetts, "For God's sake, reform the line!" Before he could say any more, Southern bullets mowed down both horse and rider. Tower turned command over to the 11th Pennsylvania's Col. Richard Coulter. "Do the best you can to hold the position, Colonel," beckoned Tower as he passed to the rear. Coulter quickly saw that all was lost.[34]

All across the eastern face of Chinn Ridge, a thick Confederate mob surged forward, driving the Federals back upon approaching Union reinforcements. Carolinians, Mississippians, Texans, and Virginians swarmed over Leppien's guns in a powerful throng. Although victorious, the charge cost the Confederates the services of General Jenkins, who was severely wounded during the attack, and of hundreds of fighting men who went down. Brigade command shifted to Col. Joseph Walker of the Palmetto Sharpshooters. Colonel Glover received a painful wound but remained in command of the 1st South Carolina.

The battle for Chinn Ridge had finally turned against the Federals. Nathaniel McLean lost nearly one-third of his men, and almost half of Tower's command fell defending the ridge. Although forced from the field, McLean and Tower achieved victory in the fight for time. Between them, they had gained nearly an hour for Pope to shore up his left. Even more important, the Federals' stiff resistance caused the Confederates to lose sight of their strategic goal—the rapid seizure of Henry Hill. Instead, the combat on Chinn Ridge sucked in the advancing Confederates and clouded their combat focus. Although forced from their position, Tower's and McLean's men had severely punished their attackers—so much so, that the Southerners would make no further headway on Chinn Ridge until fresh Confederate units renewed the attack.

Five

"We Can Keep Them Back"

THE COMBAT ON CHINN RIDGE had taken a chilling toll, and it was not yet finished. As Kemper's men battled the last vestiges of Tower's command on the ridge, still more Confederate and Federal troops moved to take part in the bloody fracas. From the south, Jones's division was swooping in toward Chinn Ridge and Henry Hill. After much delay, Law's brigade of Hood's division crept slowly through the pines screening Young's Branch.

From his headquarters on Dogan Ridge, Franz Sigel had witnessed the fighting on Chinn Ridge and saw that the Union forces there were in great need of reinforcements. Unfortunately, Sigel dispatched them in a piecemeal fashion, which negated any numerical advantage that he might have mustered had he sent the troops in together. Nevertheless, the German Americans that Sigel sent into battle on Chinn Ridge fought bravely against overwhelming odds. Their hard fighting at Second Manassas has been overlooked, while defeats at Chancellorsville and Gettysburg have been widely chronicled, even though the latter were mainly because of the untenable positions in which they had been placed rather than the troops' character.

Sigel called on Brig. Gen. Julius Stahel's brigade to supply some additional manpower. One of Stahel's regiments, Lt. Col. Ernest W. von Holmstedt's all-German 41st New York, was already in position south of the Warrenton Turnpike, with his left flank resting near Young's Branch.[1] Because of its proximity to Chinn Ridge, Sigel ordered the 41st New York into the fight. This regiment was often called the De Kalb Regiment in honor of Baron Johann de Kalb, the Bavarian officer who gave his life fighting with the Continental Army during the American Revolution at the Battle of Camden in 1780.

The 41st New York filed to the left and plunged into Young's Branch. As the New Yorkers headed toward Chinn Ridge, Capt. Robert P. Boyce's Macbeth South Carolina Artillery opened fire from the commanding heights around Groveton, making Holmstedt's task even more difficult until he could gain the cover of some intervening hills. Holmstedt's Germans then struggled up the steep and rocky northwest shoulder of Chinn Ridge and trudged through a dense pine thicket.[2]

After Sigel dispatched the 41st New York up Chinn Ridge, he directed Brig. Gen. Carl Schurz, a friend of President Abraham Lincoln, to reinforce the De Kalb Regiment with Col. John A. Koltes's brigade. Like many of Sigel's units, German immigrants and their descendants dominated the ranks of Koltes's brigade. As they descended Dogan Ridge, Stahel asked Koltes to assume command of the 41st New York, as it was too distant for the Hungarian to effectively manage. Like the 41st New York, Koltes's brigade encountered the fire of Boyce's battery as they crossed the Warrenton Turnpike and Young's Branch, and then ascended the northern shoulder of Chinn Ridge.

A few minutes after Koltes's brigade departed from Dogan Ridge, Schurz sent Col. Wlademier "Krzys" Krzyzanowski's brigade to Chinn Ridge. Krzyz had capably led this brigade in action the previous day against Maj. Gen. A. P. Hill's Light Division. The thirty-eight-year-old Krzyzanowski had participated in a failed attempt to liberate Poland from Austrian, Prussian, and Russian control in 1846. To avoid exile, Krzyzanowski fled his beloved Poland and immigrated to the United States. When the Civil War erupted in 1861, Krzyzanowski, an ardent opponent of slavery, tendered his services to the Union cause. He organized and recruited the 58th New York (the Polish Legion) and became its colonel. The unit's name served more as a tribute to Krzyzanowski's heritage than as a description of the unit's ethnic background. Like many of Sigel's units, Germans dominated the legion's ranks, but a number of Poles, Danes, Frenchmen, Italians, and Russians also served

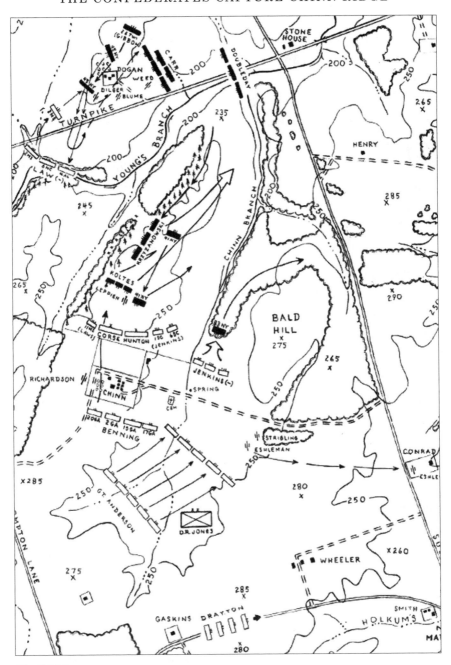

John C. McAnaw

in this cosmopolitan regiment. Although ethnically diverse, Krzyzanowski and his men shared a common ideal—a love of the freedom and opportunity that their adopted homeland had provided them.[3]

When the 41st New York reached the crest of the ridge, Holmstedt re-formed his jumbled ranks amid a shower of shot and shell. Then, the De Kalb Regiment opened fire and drove the throng of disorganized Confederates from Leppien's guns. Shortly thereafter, Koltes's brigade arrived atop Chinn Ridge and slid into position on the right flank of the 41st New York. With the 68th New York on Koltes's left flank, the 29th New York in the center, and the 73rd Pennsylvania anchoring the right flank, the brigade opened fire into the dense and jumbled masses of Kemper's division.

The 1st and 6th South Carolina of Jenkins's brigade charged, but the New Yorkers on Koltes's left forced the Confederates to seek shelter in a ravine on the side of the ridge. The 1st South Carolina's Colonel Glover, already hit once, fell mortally wounded under the Union rifle fire. As Glover was carried off the field on a blanket, he called to an officer, "You can testify that I fell with my face to the enemy," and then he wept for the slain men of his regiment.[4]

The disciplined rifle fire of Koltes's brigade and the 41st New York stunned Kemper's division, throwing it into complete confusion. Montgomery Corse rode into the midst of his retreating Virginians, grabbing the captured flag of the 11th Pennsylvania and waving it in the air. Men began to rally around him, but he soon received a painful thigh wound that forced him to drop out and left Colonel Terry in command of the brigade. "Our men began to give ground," wrote a soldier of the 17th Virginia. "On came the Yankees in splendid style, with the stars and stripes waving and their line capitally dressed." A drummer boy in front of Koltes's line beat "a pas de charge," the only time the Virginians had heard "the inspiriting sound" during war. In fact, Koltes's advance was so "perfect" that some of the Virginians became so engrossed in admiration that they forgot to fire their weapons.[5]

As the Southerners fell back, Holmstedt ordered a charge, and his Germans surged up to the guns and attempted to save them by hand. They manhandled two of the guns down the slope of ridge toward Chinn Branch.

Others loaded the guns and fired them at Kemper's stunned Confederates. Hunton's Virginians spied the 41st New York endeavoring to save the guns and fired down the valley of Chinn Branch at them. Nevertheless, the Germans persisted in their efforts to save the guns until they came under friendly fire from the Union batteries on Dogan Ridge. Unnerved, Holmstedt's men abandoned the guns between the Union and Confederate battle lines and retreated toward the Stone House. The officers attempted to rally the regiment at the base of the hill, but their efforts proved fruitless as the 41st New York had already lost 103 men in combat on the ridge.[6]

On top of the ridge, Koltes discovered a force of Confederates—probably remnants of Evans's South Carolina brigade, the 11th Mississippi, and some of Kemper's Virginians—moving through the pine thicket on the western slope of Chinn Ridge. These Southerners threatened Koltes's right flank. Reacting swiftly, the Philadelphian drew back the 73rd Pennsylvania on his right flank and traded volleys with the Southerners, parrying the Confederate thrust. Koltes's brigade and the 41st New York completed the disintegration of Kemper's division on Chinn Ridge, but the Federals' fight was not over.[7]

A decisive factor in the fight was Capt. J. B. Richardson's company of the Washington Artillery. Some of Kemper's men informed Richardson that they had previously taken Leppien's battery, but Union reinforcements had driven them off. Richardson accordingly deployed his guns in the Chinn yard just west of the house on the crest of the ridge. Then the New Orleanians hammered Koltes's regiments with "a perfect shower of projectiles." Sensing a need for action, Koltes dashed out in front of his men, "waving his sword high in the air," and ordered a charge. The command started toward the Rebel guns, but a shell exploded, its fragments striking Koltes and killing him instantly. His men rushed the guns, but the Confederate fire drove them back. Lt. John Kennedy and a few men of the 73rd Pennsylvania made it to the guns only to become prisoners, although the dashing Irishman managed to slip away in the melee. Lt. Col. Gustave A. Mulheck of the 73rd Pennsylvania took command, and in spite of Koltes's death, the brigade continued to resist the Confederate onslaught.[8]

Following Koltes to Chinn Ridge, Colonel Krzyzanowski marched his three regiments across the Warrenton Turnpike and ascended the northern shoulder of Chinn Ridge. He rode in front of his brigade as it marched into position on Koltes's right flank. The junction of these two Federal brigades formed an angle with Koltes's fronting generally south and Krzyzanowski facing west. From the pines west of Chinn Ridge, Confederates, probably from Law's brigade or Wilcox's, or both, fired at the advancing Federals. A Minié ball plunged into Krzyzanowski's horse, sending the Pole crashing to the ground headfirst and causing a severe concussion. Nevertheless, he pulled himself up and continued to lead his brigade afoot. For about fifteen minutes, Krzyzanowski's brigade dueled with the Southerners, throwing them into confusion and checking their advance. At the same time, Stahel checked the advance of Law's 2nd Mississippi near the Warrenton Turnpike. From the Chinn yard, Richardson's company of the Washington Artillery enfiladed Krzyzanowski's left flank while Boyce's battery and Law's infantry pounded the Pole's brigade from the front. Caught in a crossfire, Krzyzanowski withdrew his brigade to the shelter of the deep ravine formed by Chinn Branch near its junction with Young's Branch, while Koltes's men continued to hold Kemper's men at bay.[9]

Although Kemper's men were scattered across Chinn Ridge, Longstreet's powerful right possessed even more might with Brig. Gen. David R. "Neighbor" Jones's division. A West Point graduate, Jones had proven himself to be a capable and reliable division commander during the Seven Days Battles. His affable manner made him one of the most liked men in Lee's army, earning him the nickname "Neighbor." Although only thirty-seven, he suffered from chronic heart disease that would kill him a few months later; however, on August 30, 1862, Jones was ready for the task at hand.

Jones's division began its attack on the extreme right flank of the Confederate army near the Old Warrenton and Alexandria Road. His command contained three brigades of Georgia troops with one regiment of South Carolinians. Just prior to the advance, Colonel Rosser warned Jones that "the enemy were attempting to flank our line." Heeding this caution, Jones left Brig. Gen. Thomas F. Drayton's brigade in position to cover the army's right flank.

He went into the attack with the Georgians of Col. Henry L. Benning's and Col. George T. "Tige" Anderson's brigades. As Jones's division swung around from the right, Benning's brigade moved ahead of Anderson's, having less ground to cover in its advance. Anderson lagged shortly behind Benning, to his right and rear.[10]

Brig. Gen. Robert Toombs's Georgia brigade entered the fight on Chinn Ridge without its commander. Longstreet had placed the irascible Toombs under arrest for failure to maintain adequate security while the army was stationed along the Rappahannock River. In his stead, Benning, a former justice on the Georgia Supreme Court, led the brigade. Upon reaching the Chinn House, Benning's brigade followed the path of Corse's Virginians. On Benning's left flank, the 20th Georgia advanced past the west side of the house, while the balance of the brigade passed east of the house between it and Chinn Branch. Benning reported that this movement "caused a wide separation of the Twentieth from" the rest of the brigade. It placed the 20th Georgia atop Chinn Ridge, while the rest of the brigade advanced along lower portions of the ridge's eastern slope. When the 20th Georgia appeared on the scene, worried Confederate officers from Kemper's division rode up and cried out, "Come this way; your aid is needed; the enemy is close by."[11]

Benning overheard the commotion and galloped over to the 20th Georgia to examine the situation for himself. He immediately saw Koltes's brigade in line of battle located "a few hundred yards in our front, but a little to our left in a pine thicket." Benning then led the 20th Georgia by the left oblique (away from the rest of the brigade) and advanced through the sulfuric haze across Chinn Ridge toward the pines. Scores of scattered Mississippians, South Carolinians, Texans, and Virginians from Evans's and Kemper's divisions joined the advancing Georgians, adding weight to the renewed Confederate attack. Koltes's men fired at the Southerners, but the battle-hardened Georgians returned the fire without halting as they slowly advanced across Chinn Ridge. With Koltes lying dead on the field, his brigade shuddered before the resurgent Confederates and soon lost its cohesion.[12]

On Benning's right flank, a dense throng of Hunton's Virginians and Jenkins's South Carolinians advanced along the eastern slope of Chinn

Ridge. Krzyzanowski saw the gray coats approaching from the left and ordered his brigade back up the hill. This time, Krzyzanowski changed front to the left and shifted his troops into position where they would be better able to confront the advancing Southerners. Once in position, his New Yorkers and Pennsylvanians lashed out at the Confederates with "a well-aimed salvo," which caused those in the advance to "break up in disorder and flee." From higher up on Chinn Ridge, Capt. King Bryan of the 5th Texas saw Krzyzanowski's men and opened fire. Members of the 18th Virginia of Hunton's brigade turned the abandoned guns of Leppien's battery and fired three rounds into the Pole's brigade. The 15th and 17th Georgia moved forward on the 2nd Georgia's right flank. While they played no actual role in the fight for Chinn Ridge, their presence had a psychological impact on the Federals on the hill when they saw the Confederates moving to cut them off from the Warrenton Turnpike and Sudley Road. In the valley of Chinn Branch, the 2nd Georgia advanced several hundred yards to the 20th Georgia's right flank along the course of the stream. The 2nd entered the timber along Chinn Branch, where it halted and fired into Krzyzanowski's left flank. [13]

At the same time, Benning ordered a charge upon reaching the dense thicket. The 20th Georgia crashed into the thick tangle under a hail of musketry from Koltes's men. Without halting, the 20th Georgia and its numerous accomplices from Kemper's, Evans's, and Hood's commands returned fire at the Federals. In addition to the casualties the Southerners incurred from Union rifle fire, their bare feet added to their misery. More than a hundred men of the 20th Georgia had entered the battle with no shoes. As they pursued the retreating Federals, the Georgians charged through a heavy growth of briar. Maj. J. D. Waddell of the 20th Georgia remembered that these men "left bloody footprints among the thorns and briars through which they rushed with Spartan courage." Emerging from the thorny undergrowth, the 20th Georgia and its accomplices attacked Krzyzanowski's right flank from the ridge. Hit on both flanks, Krzyzanowski's brigade quickly fell apart. Both Union brigades, recalled Carl Schurz, "came out of the fire in a very shattered condition." [14]

When Benning's command charged the thicket, they captured Leppien's guns once again after another hand-to-hand encounter with a few diehards from the Federal ranks. "The last definite thing I remember," wrote Pvt. Alexander Hunter of the 17th Virginia, "were those wild men in gray crowding up to the batteries, some foaming at the mouth—they had run mad for the time." The whole scene about the guns was "so violent and tempestuous, so mad and brain-reeling that to recall it is like fixing the memory of a horrible, blood-curdling dream," he recalled. Then as suddenly as it began, "the mists dissolved and the panting, grasping soldiers" regained their sanity and realized what had happened: they had captured the battery.[15]

Koltes's brigade had fought a valiant, albeit futile, delaying action against an overwhelming Confederate force, and its casualties reflected this effort. The 68th New York lost its commander, Lt. Col. John H. Kleefisch, to a mortal wound. Additionally, the unit lost thirteen men killed, sixty-three wounded, and twenty-one captured during its fight on Chinn Ridge. The 73rd Pennsylvania suffered even more. One hundred and twenty-nine men were killed or wounded, and twenty-eight captured or missing. Twenty-seven men of the 41st New York were killed outright on Chinn Ridge, while another sixty suffered wounds. In two days of combat, the 29th New York lost one hunderd and fifty men killed, wounded, or captured, with many of the losses occurring on Chinn Ridge. Clearly, Koltes's brigade and the 41st New York made a great sacrifice to buy fifteen or so minutes for Pope to secure his avenue of retreat, which he had ironically cared for so little when he first assumed command of the Army of Virginia.

Although often overlooked, Koltes's and Krzyzanowski's brigades played a crucial role in preventing the Confederate seizure of the Stone House intersection. With the 41st New York, Koltes's brigade stopped Kemper's division cold after its success against Tower and McLean, driving the Southerners away from Leppien's battery. Krzyzanowski's brigade prevented Law's Confederates from striking Koltes's right flank on his first sally. After falling back, Krzyzanowski saw the Confederates pressing forward on the left, so he marched his brigade back up Chinn Ridge and changed front to meet the Southerners, shutting off the most direct route to the Stone House intersection. Without these efforts by Koltes and Krzyzanowski, the Confederates might have seized the crossroad and split Pope's Army of Virginia in half, rendering untold damage.

After almost two hours of combat, Longstreet finally possessed Chinn Ridge in its entirety. The opportunity to irreparably harm the Federal army by catching the bulk of Pope's army north of Warrenton Turnpike had slipped from his grasp, however. Hood's and Evans's brigades were by and large done fighting for the day, as were Corse's and Hunton's Virginians. At least one half of Jenkins's South Carolinians took no further part in the battle. It would be up to Neighbor Jones, a few Texans, and some of Jenkins's men to carry the battle into its next phase, until Wilcox and Lee's reserves (Gen. Richard H. Anderson's division) could enter the fray.

DOGAN RIDGE

While Benning's Georgians cleared Chinn Ridge, Col. Evander Law's brigade, minus the 11th Mississippi, arrived on the heights where the Texas Brigade overran Kerns's battery. Law saw Federals deploying in a ravine and positioned his men to counter them. With the 6th North Carolina on the right flank, 4th Alabama in the center, and 2nd Mississippi on the left, Law's brigade advanced into a pine thicket on the south bank of Young's Branch. Although Law believed that the 11th Mississippi was moving into position north of the Warrenton Turnpike to attack Sigel on Dogan Ridge, Liddell had instead led it to the right where it had stumbled into the action around the Chinn House. To support this intended flanking movement, Law ordered the 2nd Mississippi to attack Sigel's position from the south side of the pike. Crossing Young's Branch, the 2nd Mississippi emerged from the pines in the open ground at the southwestern base of Dogan Ridge.

At the time of Law's advance, only Col. George von Amsberg's 45th New York of Stahel's brigade and Capt. Hubert Dilger's and Lt. Theodore Blume's batteries remained in position near the Dogan House; they fired away at the Confederates advancing south of the turnpike. The balance of Sigel's troops withdrew down a dirt lane, leading toward Buck Hill. Amsberg's 45th New York occupied the ground immediately north of the Dogan House, fronting westward. When the 2nd Mississippi emerged from the pines to the south, Amsberg deftly changed front to the left to meet the Confederates charging up Dogan Ridge. His Germans moved into the garden and formed their battle line along the fence fronting southward. The Germans delivered a "well aimed fire" by file into the 2nd Mississippi while Dilger's and Blume's gunners shredded the Southern ranks with canister. In a matter of minutes, the 2nd Mississippi lost twenty-two men killed and eighty-seven wounded; Amsberg reported that the field was "covered with the dead and wounded."[16]

He then ordered a countercharge, and the 45th New York surged down the southwest slope of Dogan Ridge led by Lt. Col. Edward Wratislaw, driving the remnants of the 2nd Mississippi back into the pine thickets and capturing some prisoners. "With rejoicing and cheers, we follow over the fence and ditches, down into the valley until the enemy disappears in the brush," according to Louis Biskey of the 45th New York. The situation turned for the worse when the 45th New York reached the open ground surrounding the Warrenton Turnpike. A bullet struck Wratislaw's horse, and the regiment surged ahead of him, losing cohesion as it rapidly pursued the Mississippians. While the Mississippians retreated, the 6th North Carolina and 4th Alabama waited at the edge of the thicket with their rifles at the ready for their comrades to clear out of the field. When they did, the North Carolinians and Alabamans fired a volley into the spread-out 45th New York, checking its advance. The New Yorkers' sudden appearance in the open ground also elicited deadly fire from the Confederate batteries posted on the heights near Groveton, which sent the Federals reeling in confusion up Dogan Ridge, through Dilger's battery, and into the orchard.[17]

When the New Yorkers exited the east end of the orchard, they encountered Brig. Gen. John B. Gibbon's Black Hat Brigade, which had suffered enormous losses at Brawner's Farm on August 28. Gibbon halted the shell-shocked 45th New York by having his Wisconsin troops level their bayonets. He ordered the New Yorkers back to the front, but they refused to go, having already been there once and forced to leave with heavy losses. Realizing the futility of the situation, Gibbon turned to the men of the consolidated 2nd/7th Wisconsin and said, "Men, will you go?" The hearty Wisconsin men responded with cheers. An officer rode out in front of them and shouted, "Come on, boys, God damn them! We can keep them back."[18]

As Gibbon's men marched into the orchard, Law's brigade charged up the southwest face of Dogan Ridge toward Dilger's Ohio battery. The 4th

Alabama and 6th North Carolina moved toward Dilger's guns, and the Wisconsin men posted in the nearby orchard. The Southerners fired two volleys into the Ohioans, and Dilger limbered his guns and fell back a hundred yards. Dilger was not done fighting, however. Instead the German rapidly redeployed his battery for action and raked the Southerners with canister. At the same time, Gibbon's Black Hats laced the Rebels with a deadly volley from their rifles that made it too hot for Law's men to sustain their position. Under both artillery and small arms fire, the Confederates abandoned Dogan Ridge for the safety of the low ground. True to their word, Gibbon's Wisconsin men, with the assistance of Captain Dilger, had indeed held off Law's brigade north of the Warrenton Turnpike. [19]

The Union troops had repelled the Confederate attempts to capture Dogan Ridge, thus securing the vital intersection in front of the Stone House. This was crucial, for large parts of Pope's army were still falling back from their positions north and west of the intersection. If the Confederates had gained control of the commanding heights of Dogan Ridge at this time, their artillery could have turned Pope's retreat into a confused rout reminiscent of the distressing scenes that followed the First Battle of Bull Run. But the combined efforts of the Union infantry and artillery on Dogan Ridge allowed for a more orderly withdrawal.

The German artillerists under Captain Dilger played an integral role in the successful Union defense on Dogan Ridge, his battery being the only unit engaged in both repulses. Schurz called him "one of the most brilliant artillery officers in our army." Indeed he was. Dilger consistently bore out the truth of Schurz's praise on the fields of Chancellorsville, Gettysburg, and throughout the 1864 Atlanta Campaign of Maj. Gen. William T. Sherman. His battery was the last Federal unit to leave Dogan Ridge. As Dilger pulled back, he twice halted to blast back pursuing Confederates before continuing the retreat. Then, under orders from Schurz, he deployed two guns to cover the bridge that carried the Warrenton Turnpike across Young's Branch. [20]

As the Union soldiers retreated along the Warrenton Turnpike, the Confederate artillery sent solid shot and shell into its blue ranks. "It is a pitiful sight to see man or beast struck with one of those terrible things," wrote a

Massachusetts soldier. "That terrified look of surprise on the face of man—the upraised quivering arms and slow dropping of them to the side—makes a man sick. 'Oh-God' comes to a man's lips unconsciously."[21]

SUDLEY ROAD

While the combat roared on Chinn Ridge, Pope established a tenuous battle line toward the east and across Sudley Road on Henry Hill. Pope and McDowell halted any troops they came across and ordered them to the beleaguered left flank. Earlier on Dogan Ridge, Brig. Gen. George Sykes had noted the natural strength of Henry Hill and suggested to Maj. Gen. Fitz John Porter that Sykes's Regular brigades occupy "the plateau of the Henry and Robinson houses beyond Young's Run." Porter consented, and Sykes's Regulars were on their way to aid in saving the Army of Virginia from further damage. From Henry Hill, Pope spied Sykes's lead unit, Lt. Col. William Chapman's brigade, marching east on the turnpike. Pope galloped after the Regulars, reined in his horse, and called out to the rear regiment of Chapman's column, "What troops are these and where are you going?" "To Bull Run Hill," answered Maj. George L. Andrews, commander of the 17th U.S. Infantry. What Andrews referred to as Bull Run Hill was actually Henry Hill. By misnaming the heights to which he was headed, Andrews gave Pope the impression that the Regulars were retreating to the hills overlooking Bull Run. Consequently, Pope "soundly berated" Andrews and ordered them to halt where they were, and then rode away. Shortly thereafter, McDowell rode up and peremptorily ordered Andrews to take his unit to the extreme left of the Federal line, and the balance of Chapman's brigade followed.[22]

Chapman's brigade hurried across Henry Farm and followed Sudley Road through the timber south of the house to the open plain beyond. No sooner had the 17th U.S. emerged from the woods than one of Rosser's batteries blasted the Regulars back into the forest. There, Chapman deployed the consolidated 2nd/10th U.S. Infantry Battalion in line of battle along Sudley Road, a washed-out road cut that provided a natural breastwork for the troops. Andrews then posted the 17th U.S. on the left flank of the consolidated 2nd/10th U.S. battalion. On the right flank of the consolidated battalion, Chapman advanced the 6th U.S. Infantry into the woods west of the road. Maj. Delancey Floyd-Jones's 11th U.S. Infantry anchored Chapman's right flank, supported by a section from Capt. Albert Monroe's Battery D, 1st Rhode Island Light Artillery. Capt. John W. Ames of the 11th U.S. Infantry felt confident that the Regulars could hold this position. He wrote, "Our fear had all gone; we examined our musket-locks; shoved cartridge boxes round to the front of our belts and picked out such slim shelter as the shallow roadside ditch could afford."[23]

Col. Robert Buchanan's brigade had followed Chapman to Henry Hill. He posted his five U.S. Regular Army infantry battalions immediately south of the burned-out remains of the old Henry House. The 3rd U.S. anchored Buchanan's right flank on the house itself. The 4th and 14th U.S. continued the battle line to the left. The 12th U.S. held the Regulars' left flank. Higher up on the hill, the 20-pounder Parrotts of Captain Hall's 2nd Maine Battery added their weight to the patchwork Union battle line. The presence of Pope and McDowell along the Henry Hill and Sudley Road battle line did not go unnoticed. "If brains and military skill were wanting in our leaders," a soldier of the 11th U.S. Infantry recalled, "personal bravery certainly was not. Let us be fair about this! General officers and staff officers were galloping all over the ground—close to the enemy's skirmish line as it seemed to us."[24]

As previously noted, Pope had already ordered Brig. Gen. Robert H. Milroy's Independent Brigade of West Virginians and Ohioans into the woods on the southern fringe of Henry Hill. Milroy had matriculated at Norwich Military Academy in Vermont, the northern equivalent of the Virginia Military Institute, where he learned the art of war. Milroy was also one of the Union's more unusual characters and an aggressive Indiana abolitionist. One soldier described Milroy as a general who "will hunt up the enemy and fight him wherever found." Another ranked him "among the first generals in the field for bravery and fight." And fight he would with his own and any other troops he could obtain, much to the annoyance of his fellow generals.[25]

Milroy found Chapman's brigade deployed in the wooded stretch of Sudley Road that Pope had referred to, so the Hoosier posted his Independent

Brigade in the cut formed by the road on Chapman's right flank. Shaped by the course of the road, Milroy's battle line was concave, with his right flank resting near the lane that led from the road up the hill to the Henry House. His left extended toward Chapman's right flank in the hardwood forest that wrapped around Bald Hill. The 5th West Virginia anchored Milroy's right flank, and the 82nd Ohio held the slightly advanced center of the arching battle line. Milroy's troops enjoyed the luxury of fighting from the three- to six-feet-deep road cut. Capt. Albert Monroe's Battery D, 1st Rhode Island Light Artillery, unlimbered behind Milroy on the western slope of Henry Hill.

Under Pope's personal direction, Brig. Gen. John F. Reynolds moved his two remaining brigades of Pennsylvania Reserves to Henry Hill and deployed them in a double line of battle immediately north of the house where "shot and shell flew like hail." Brig. Gen. George G. Meade's brigade occupied the front line with Brig. Gen. Truman Seymour's forming the second line of battle. The 8th Pennsylvania Reserves held Meade's left flank, while the 13th Reserves, the Bucktails, manned the right end. In front of the infantry, Reynolds posted Capt. Dunbar Ransom's Battery C, 5th U.S. Artillery.

The South Carolinians of Jenkins's right wing (2nd Rifles, 5th Infantry, and Palmetto Sharpshooters), now commanded by Col. Joseph Walker of the Palmetto Sharpshooters, charged over Bald Hill and into the woods separating it from Sudley Road. Captain Bryan of the 5th Texas saw the South Carolinians enter the timber and hurried his remaining Texans into position on Jenkins's left flank. These Southern troops picked their way through the woods and pine thickets west of Sudley Road toward Henry Hill, driving out hundreds of Federals who had taken refuge in the woods and were attempting to slow the Confederate advance. Then, South Carolinians and Texans pressed on, with their sights set on capturing the Union artillery on Henry Hill.[26]

As the Union soldiers lay in the weathered road cut, they could see nothing through the trees but heard the reverberating sounds of battle creeping ever nearer. Suddenly, a "tempest of bullets" chased great crowds of retreating Federals from the woods and whizzed harmlessly over the heads of the entrenched Unionists. Some of the retreating Federals stopped and rallied on the Sudley Road line, including such survivors from the Chinn Ridge fight as Col. Orland Smith's 73rd Ohio and Lt. Col. Gustave Mulheck's 73rd Pennsylvania. The remaining diehards from the two 73rd regiments joined the Union battle line between Chapman's right and Milroy's left. The 83rd New York of Stiles's brigade emerged from the woods farther to the south, and went into position in the road and extended the line southward from Chapman's left flank.[27]

With a "rattling crash of musketry" and a "screaming yell of men," Colonel Walker's Palmetto Sharpshooters and Col. John V. Moore's 2nd South Carolina Rifles stormed out of the pines and headed toward a rail fence between the road and the trees. Before they could reach the fence line, the 11th U.S., the twin 73s, and the Independent Brigade opened fire. From the rise behind the road, Captain Monroe's Napoleons spewed canister into the Confederate ranks. "We . . . made it quite lively for them," recalled Capt. John Ames of the 11th U.S., "for they never reached the fence in front." "The clash of arms [was] terrific—the carnage appalling," noted Pvt. William R. Rankin of the Palmetto Sharpshooters. On Walker's left flank, the 5th South Carolina cut its losses and halted behind a rail fence at the edge of the woods, firing back at Milroy's West Virginians "as fast as we could load."[28]

From the road cut, Milroy's West Virginians and Ohioans wielded their rifles with deadly effect. The attacking South Carolinians and Texans "tumbled and melted away," a sight Milroy found "most beautiful and cheering." One of Milroy's regiments, the 82nd Ohio, had suffered severe casualties during the fighting on August 29. Its losses included the regiment's popular commander, Col. James Cantwell, who was killed leading an attack against Stonewall Jackson's wing. On August 30, Maj. David Thompson of the 82nd Ohio rode his battle line, cheering the men while defying the "the tremendous fire" pouring out of the woods. Shouting the battle cry of "Remember Cantwell," the sweaty and powder-grimed soldiers of the 82nd Ohio fired their rifles into the Confederates and "paid them" for the heavy losses of the previous day.[29]

With no chance of success, the 5th Texas, 5th South Carolina, 2nd South Carolina Rifles, and Palmetto Sharpshooters "were forced to secede" from their position and retreat "a respectful distance" into the woods. Captain Bryan of the 5th Texas was carried from the field with a severe wound. The 2nd South Carolina Rifles lost Colonel Moore to a mortal wound. Scores of other Texans and South Carolinians lay dead and wounded near the tree line. Nevertheless, the 5th South Carolina remained ensconced behind the rail fence and trees at the edge of the woods, firing away until their rifles "got so hot we had to wait for them to cool." Although the 5th South Carolina held its position, the attack had failed to break the Union battle line. Yet Confederate reinforcements would renew the conflict without interruption as Brig. Gen. David Jones's division carried on the fight.[30]

Jones's keen eye took in the situation, and he realized that significant damage could still be inflicted upon Pope's army if the Confederate forces rapidly seized Henry Hill. To this end, Jones ordered Brig. Gen. Thomas F. Drayton to "completely sweep" around the Federal left flank with his two-thousand-man brigade. At the same time, Benning's and Tige Anderson's brigades would hit the Sudley Road line from the front. Unfortunately for the Confederate cause, Drayton was an incompetent field officer who owed his position to an old West Point comrade, Confederate president Jefferson Davis. Drayton failed to promptly carry out his orders. "Again and again did I send for Drayton," lamented Jones, but rumors of a supposedly menacing Union cavalry force on the Confederate right froze the timid Drayton in place. Lacking the flanking maneuver, Jones's brilliantly conceived attack degenerated into a brutal, head-on frontal assault.[31]

Benning's Georgians of Jones's division arrived in front of Henry Hill as the first wave of Confederate attackers receded before the Federal breakwall along Sudley Road. Benning's brigade approached the road, his battle line creating an acute angle with the road. Maj. Jesse H. Pickett's 17th Georgia anchored Benning's right flank and formed the vertex of the angle. As Pickett's Georgians emerged from the woods, the 5th West Virginia on Milroy's right flank opened fire. The 82nd Ohio poured several deadly volleys into the 17th Georgia's exposed left flank, forcing it to retreat to the cover of the woods once more. There, the Georgians lay down and fired back at the Federals. One Georgian explained, "Our regiment was exposed to the hottest

D. R. JONES ATTACKS SUDLEY ROAD AND HENRY HILL

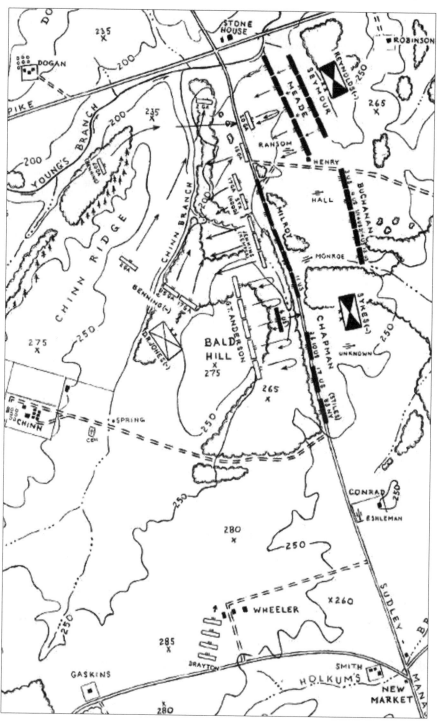

John C. McAnaw

fire, from 4 o'clock p. m., until dark. We maintained our position against four regiments for more than two hours, not giving back a foot." Although the 17th Georgia maintained its ground, the attack had failed to break the Union battle line along Sudley Road.[32]

To the left of the 17th Georgia, the 15th Georgia trampled through the smoke-filled woods east of Chinn Branch amid blasts of canister from Monroe's battery on Henry Hill. The 5th West Virginia fired into the Georgians as they moved obliquely toward Sudley Road, but failed to check their advance. The 15th Georgia exited the woods north of Milroy's position and dashed forward to occupy a vacant stretch of Sudley Road in front of the Henry House. Reaching the edge of the woods, the 15th sprinted forward and seized the stretch of Sudley Road off to Milroy's right in front of Reynolds's Pennsylvania Reserves. There, they lay down and fired at the Federals on the hill. The 15th Georgia's right flank rested on the crest of Henry Hill and extended down the hill's northern slope toward Young's Branch.

Farther north, Benning and the 20th Georgia charged the unoccupied stretch of Sudley Road to the left of the 15th Georgia. He had remained with the 20th Georgia on the extreme left of his brigade as it swept across Chinn Ridge. Reaching the northeast shoulder of the ridge, Benning halted his small force at the edge of a pine thicket and scanned the Federal position on Henry Hill, almost a thousand yards distant. Seeing the damage the Ransom's battery was inflicting upon the Confederates, Benning turned to his men and said, "Boys, we must get them damn fellows away from yonder." Benning ordered a charge, and the 20th Georgia—joined singly and in small groups by Texans, Virginians, South Carolinians, and Mississippians—surged down Chinn Ridge and crossed the valley of Chinn Branch. Halting on the eastern bank of the branch, Benning shouted, "Lay down boys. Damn hard job." Sheltered by the steep slope, the men of the 20th Georgia stopped and caught their breaths at the base of the hill for five minutes while "a terrific storm of missiles" passed just over their heads. After a brief respite, Benning ordered the 20th Georgia to "rise and take the battery." The Georgians scampered up the slope and surged toward Sudley Road.[33]

Prior to the 20th Georgia's attack on Henry Hill, Lt. Col. W. R. Holmes's 2nd Georgia had pursued retreating Federals through the trees along the eastern bank of Chinn Branch while the 20th Georgia swept Chinn Ridge. In the process, Holmes's Georgians passed beyond the 20th Georgia and became the extreme left flank of Benning's brigade. The 2nd Georgia guided its advance on the Stone House and closed in on that crossroad at the heart of Pope's army. At last, it looked as though Longstreet might gain the long-sought seizure of the strategic heights of Henry Hill and the intersection.

On top of Henry Hill, Capt. Dunbar Ransom of the 5th U.S. Artillery saw the menacing Georgians burst from their cover and exclaimed, "They're coming, boys!" He barked to the men who were carrying ammunition from the caissons to the guns, "Nothing but case shot—bring nothing but case shot!" Behind Dunbar, Pennsylvania's Brig. Gen. John F. Reynolds turned to his men and bellowed, "Now, boys! Give them the steel! Charge bayonets double quick!" Even the normally dour Brig. Gen. George G. Meade grew "almost excited" as he led his brigade of Pennsylvania Reserves down the western slope of Henry Hill in a headlong charge. Brig. Gen. Truman Seymour, commanding Reynolds's second line, gently waved his hand to signal his brigade to advance. Meade's impetuous advance drove the 15th and 20th Georgia back into the woods. Benning lamented, "Heavy infantry supports . . . now became visible. . . . It would be madness to let the regiment go on." So Benning ordered the 20th Georgia to retreat to the safety of Chinn Branch ravine. From there, the Georgians kept up a fire at Reynolds's Pennsylvanians.[34]

Reynolds's men did not halt when they reached Sudley Road. Instead, they charged into the woods and pine thickets where they encountered heavy musket fire from the 15th and 20th Georgia. Lieutenant Colonel Holmes of the 2nd Georgia saw the Pennsylvanians charge down Henry Hill. At that instant, the 2nd Georgia had advanced to within 250 yards of the Stone House. Seeing the Pennsylvanians advancing on his right rear, Holmes halted the 2nd Georgia, changed front to the right, and opened fire upon the Reserve's right flank. The Georgians' volley hit the Pennsylvanians like a lightning bolt. One of Meade's men thought they had entered "the fire of hell, completely enveloped in smoke and flame." The musketry of Benning's brigade "literally whirled" the Pennsylvanians back up the slope of Henry Hill.[35]

Just when the Reserves appeared to be on the verge of fleeing the field entirely, the inspiring leadership of Reynolds and Meade staved off a complete break. With canister from Ransom's guns holding off the Georgians, Reynolds grabbed the tattered flag of the 6th Reserves. He furiously galloped along his splintered battle line, waving it above his head, "infusing into the men a spirit to do anything else but run." Electrified by Reynolds's display of valor, the Pennsylvania Reserves rallied in the cut of Sudley Road and fired back at the Georgians. An intense firefight ensued between the Pennsylvanians in the road cut and the Georgians in the woods, but the more numerous Pennsylvanians held the Southerners at bay, preventing Longstreet from seizing the Stone House intersection.[36]

Although Reynolds had secured the crossroads, the battle continued with increasing fury farther south on Sudley Road. There, Col. George Anderson's Georgia brigade from Jones's division threatened to crush the Federal left flank and take Henry Hill. If it succeeded, Confederate artillery on the hill could severely damage Pope's army, greatly increasing Federal casualties and adding confusion to an otherwise orderly retreat. Its commander, Colonel Anderson, had served in the Mexican War and earned a captain's commission in the U.S. Regular Army, in which he served until 1859, proving himself to be a steady and competent officer.

Anderson advanced with the 8th Georgia manning his right flank. The 1st Georgia Regulars and 7th and 9th Georgia extended the line to the left in that order. The 11th Georgia, led by Lt. Col. William Luffman, anchored the brigade's left flank during the advance. When Anderson's men received the order to advance, Col. William T. "Billy" Wilson stood in front of the 7th Georgia, which had earned a solid reputation at First Manassas. "Boys," called Wilson, "we have come back to our old stomping ground. If any of you kill a Yankee, put on his shoes quick and if you get into a sutler store, eat all the cheese and crackers you can possibly hold. And, if you get any good cigars, give old Billy two. Forward!"[37]

Anderson had followed Benning's brigade onto the battlefield and swung its right flank around, then went into the line of battle to the right and rear of Benning. Anderson's men passed well east of the Chinn House.

The 11th Georgia on their left passed over Chinn Spring as it made its way up Bald Hill under artillery fire from the Federal batteries on Henry Hill. As Anderson's Georgians crested Bald Hill, the 6th U.S., posted in the woods west of Sudley Road, opened fire. The Georgians replied with a withering fire into the Regulars' front and both flanks. The Georgians charged toward the woods, and the soldiers of the 6th U.S. "instinctively retired behind the fence along the road," losing several men in the process.[38]

While Milroy's Independent Brigade and the U.S. Regulars waited in the shelter of the road cut, the Confederate rifle fire "told with destructive results" on Captain Monroe's exposed Rhode Island battery. One of Rosser's batteries on the Confederate right ranged in perfectly on the Rhode Island-ers, showering the Federal gunners with shrapnel. The gunners grew uneasy at their situation and prepared to withdraw. Like an apparition, Milroy burst into the midst of the Rhode Islanders "with sword in one hand and his hat in the other," cheering the gunners on and urging them to stand their ground. A bullet killed Milroy's horse, but the brigadier jumped atop his saddle and ordered the gunners to fire canister into the woods. The Rhode Islanders' "big guns vomited sheets of canister into that forest." Milroy opined that it "appeared to be full of rebels and from the tremendous storm of bullets we poured into that forest, I did not see how any could escape, but still the deadly shower that came out of that forest seemed rather to increase rather than abate."[39]

No sooner had Milroy rallied the gunners than the 73rd Ohio and Penn-sylvania regiments abandoned the road cut and joined the retreating 6th U.S. Infantry. From his perch atop Henry Hill with the Rhode Island artil-lery, Milroy observed the confusion and roared into action. He sped toward the retreating Ohioans, waving his arms energetically and shouting epithets such as "hell and chickens." To Milroy's surprise, the Ohioans obeyed his or-ders "with more alacrity than any other strange troops before." Then Milroy realized that the troops involved belonged to Smith's 73rd Ohio, a unit that had served under Milroy in the Shenandoah Valley and West Virginia earlier in the year. With the Ohioans back in the road cut firing at the Southerners in the woods, Milroy dashed back to the right, where he found his Indepen-dent Brigade "holding their position and working splendidly."[40]

Col. Leopold von Gilsa's 41st New York Infantry was recruited among the German immigrant community of New York City and two companies of Germans from Philadelphia. In the struggle for Chinn Ridge, twenty-seven of them were killed, sixty wounded, and sixteen missing as they battled for the preservation of their adopted country. (Library of Congress)

Col. Jerome B. Robertson commanded the 5th Texas Infantry at the Second Battle of Manassas, where his regiment spearheaded Longstreet's attack. This Kentucky native moved to Texas in 1836 and served in the Republic of Texas's army as a captain. He commanded the famous Texas Brigade of the Army of Northern Virginia for much of the war, including the Battle of Gettysburg. (Library of Congress)

Gen. David R. Jones was a native of South Carolina and nephew of former U.S. president Zachary Taylor. Jones graduated from West Point in 1846, and his guiding hand played a key role in Lee's victory at Second Manassas. He died of a heart ailment in early 1863, robbing the Confederacy of a most capable division commander. (Library of Congress)

German-born Gen. Franz Sigel commanded the I Corps of Pope's Army of Virginia. Sigel was popular among both the German-born and native soldiers who served under him throughout the war, although his popularity did not translate into success on the battlefield. (Library of Congress)

Gen. John B. Hood gained a reputation for being a ferocious combat general as a brigade and division commander in the Army of Northern Virginia. He would lose an arm at Gettysburg and a leg at Chickamauga in 1863 before going on to lead the Confederate Army of Tennessee in the latter part of the Atlanta Campaign of 1864. (Library of Congress)

Gen. Irvin McDowell commanded the defeated Union army at the First Battle of Manassas in 1861, and his actions in 1862 contributed to Pope's defeat at Second Manassas. (Library of Congress)

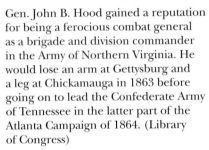

Col. John H. Means was a former governor of South Carolina who had long advocated separation from the North. When war came, he enlisted as a private in the 17th South Carolina and was promptly elected colonel, an office he held until his death at Second Manassas. (United States Army Military History Institute)

Col. John A. Koltes, commander of a brigade in Sigel's corps who was killed attempting to drive the Confederates from Chinn Ridge. (Library of Congress)

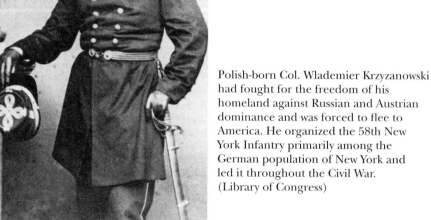

Polish-born Col. Wlademier Krzyzanowski had fought for the freedom of his homeland against Russian and Austrian dominance and was forced to flee to America. He organized the 58th New York Infantry primarily among the German population of New York and led it throughout the Civil War. (Library of Congress)

The wiry Gen. William Mahone went down wounded in front of the final Union position on Henry Hill as he led his Virginians forward in an assault. (Library of Congress)

The son of a Supreme Court Justice who dissented with the Dred Scott decision, Col. Nathaniel C. McLean commanded the Ohio Brigade that was left to fend for itself only moments before Longstreet launched his attack. His actions and those of his men likely saved Pope's army from irreparable damage. (Library of Congress)

Maj. Gen. James Longstreet, known as Robert E. Lee's War Horse, was the architect of the attack that gained victory for the Army of Northern Virginia at Second Manassas. (Library of Congress)

Maj. Gen. John Pope had served in the west under Gen. Henry Halleck and was brought east based largely on the merits of his victory at the Battle of Island No. 10 on the Mississippi River. (Library of Congress)

In August of 1862, Gen. Robert E. Lee had been in command of the Army of Northern Virginia for less than three months. He had saved Richmond from capture earlier that summer with a series of sledgehammer attacks that had cost the Confederacy dearly in terms of casualties. The Second Manassas Campaign provided Lee with his first opportunity to achieve a decisive victory through maneuver and aggressiveness that nearly decimated Pope's army. (Library of Congress)

Brig. Gen. Robert Schenck was no stranger to the plains of Manassas. The leading poker expert of his day and congressman from Ohio had led a brigade at the First Battle of Manassas in 1861. A severe wound received in the combat on Chinn Ridge ended his field service. (Library of Congress)

Three Union defenders who resisted Longstreet's Attack: On the left, Col. Governeur K. Warren; third from left, Brig. Gen. George G. Meade of the Pennsylvania Reserves; on far right, commander of the U.S. Regular Division, Brig. Gen. George Sykes. (Library of Congress)

Brig. Gen. Cadmus M. Wilcox led his brigade in the final attacks against Henry Hill. His performance at Second Manassas disappointed Longstreet, as he arrived late in the attack after misconstruing his orders. (Library of Congress)

Maj. Gen. James E. B. Stuart commanded Lee's cavalry at Second Manassas but also played a key role in keeping the Confederate artillery racing forward on the extreme right so that it played a significant part in ending Union resistance on the afternoon of August 30. (Library of Congress)

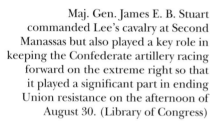

Alfred Waud sketched this scene of the Union infantry on the left of the battle line resisting Longstreet's attack late in the afternoon of August 30, 1862. The pencils and sketchpads of artists such as Waud sufficed for the combat chroniclers of the Civil War era. (Library of Congress)

After driving the 6th U.S., Anderson quickly pressed his brigade forward and assaulted Chapman's brigade, hoping to force it from the road cut. "Knock them the hell out of their damn blue shirts," yelled Anderson. On his right flank, the 8th Georgia charged the 17th U.S. and 83rd New York on the extreme left of the Union battle line. The New Yorkers overlapped the Georgians' right and raked their flank with a deadly enfilading fire, and the 8th Georgia recoiled back into the woods, where Anderson promptly refused his right flank to prevent further damage. On the 8th's left flank, the 1st Georgia Regulars confronted the 2nd/10th Consolidated Battalion of U.S. Regulars, who received them "in warm style." Under a fusillade from the Regulars, the Georgians lay on the ground, "every man shooting for all he was worth, looking like a solid sheet of flames from their guns." The 7th Georgia struck the 6th U.S. after it settled into position along the road cut, but fared no better than the rest of the brigade. Col. Benjamin Beck's 9th Georgia tramped through the woods and delivered a crashing volley into the 11th U.S. The Georgians burst toward a fence separating the two sides but never made it. One big Southerner did make it to the fence without being shot and climbed to the top. Then a Federal bullet struck him; the Georgian sat there, straddling the fence, "swaying back and forth, till he fell heavily inside." On the hill behind the Regulars, the Rhode Island gunners danced "with excitement and delight" as their canister shredded Anderson's ranks. Every time Monroe's guns fired, the men of the 11th U.S. ducked down as the canister sailed overhead. Even so, "burning bits of flannel and great puffs of hot smoke" covered the Regulars with ash and soot.

On Anderson's left flank, Luffman's 11th Georgia hit Smith's bloodied and exhausted 73rd Ohio and the other troops who had rallied in the road cut among Milroy's men. These Federals fired their last rounds and then abandoned the position. Despite the break, the fire of Chapman's Regulars on the right, Milroy's West Virginians on the left, and the batteries on Henry Hill prevented the 11th Georgia from exploiting the breach. Farther north, 82nd Ohio and 5th West Virginia of Milroy's brigade continued their battle with the 5th South Carolina and 17th Georgia, while Reynolds's Pennsylvanians continued keep the balance of Benning's brigade pinned down. As the

Southerners renewed their efforts against Milroy's men, Lt. Col. James Robinson of the 82nd Ohio galloped into the maelstrom. Although he was serving as Sigel's provost marshal, Robinson left the safety of the rear to be with his comrades on the firing line. Robinson dashed back and forth along the battle line, waving his sword in the air and cheering the men on, "perfectly insensible to the danger he was in." At one point, the bluish-gray smoke became so heavy that Milroy ordered his men to cease firing. As soon as the smoke cleared, his West Virginians and Ohioans again sent "their volleys of thunder and death" into the Confederates, leaving the ground "thickly sprinkled" with their dead and wounded.[41]

Although the Union battle line was holding out, the troops in the road cut were under increasing pressure and their ammunition was running out. Confidence in the Army of Virginia's leadership had been skeptical even before Pope's blunders of August 30, and men began to drift away from the firing line. This leakage necessitated that reinforcements be sent if the Federals were to hold the line at Henry Hill. To meet this need, McDowell ordered Brig. Gen. A. Sanders Piatt to Milroy's support. After erroneously marching to Centreville and back earlier in the day, Piatt's men had waited in line of battle behind the Regulars and Pennsylvania Reserves in the open fields of Henry Hill. Suddenly, an orderly dashed up and ordered the 86th New York to bolster Chapman's brigade, which was "beginning to give way." Leaving the 63rd Indiana to support some unspecified artillery on the hill, Piatt double-quicked the 86th New York (Steuben Rangers) across the open fields of Henry Hill, with shells from Stribling's and Eshleman's guns crashing in from the south and exploding all around them. One New Yorker proudly wrote, "On went the regiment over and down the hill, quickly closing up the ranks as fast as the men fell out, wounded or killed." The Rangers charged down the hill toward the woods, halted on the embankment behind the 6th and 11th U.S., and opened fire just as some of Anderson's Georgians once again emerged from the opposite woods and attempted to force Chapman's brigade from its position in road cut. Sixty-one-year-old Col. Benajah P. Bailey yelled to his Rangers, "Give it to them, boys, stand by the colors."[42]

Although Anderson's Georgians retreated into the woods, they halted and fired back at the bluecoats from the high ground opposite the 86th New

York. Unlike Milroy's and Chapman's troops, the Steuben Rangers stood atop the bank behind the road cut, where the Confederates "poured a shower of Minnie balls" into them. The New Yorkers endured the punishment until orders came to fall back from their unprotected position. By then the damage had been done; in a short span of time, the Steuben Rangers had lost more than a hundred men killed and wounded.[43]

When the 73rd Ohio and others abandoned the road cut on Milroy's left, they "rushed pell-mell" through the guns and limbers of Monroe's Rhode Island battery. Believing that the entire Sudley Road line was about to crumble, the Rhode Island gunners fell back to avoid their perceived capture. Lieutenant Colonel Chapman of the Regulars complained that the battery "limbered to the rear and left its position at the very moment when it could have done excellent service." Chapman continued, "The enemy's musketry was not sufficiently dangerous enough to drive him off, and he had the infantry support of my entire brigade."[44]

Anderson's Georgians suffered horrendously under the firestorm pouring into the pine woods west of Sudley Road. Federal slugs and bullets killed and wounded more than six hundred of Anderson's men, the 11th Georgia alone losing almost two hundred. Anderson had his gray horse shot out from under him. The 11th's Capt. Matthew Nunnelly later declared, "I was never in an engagement so terrible as this." Nunnelly's company battled the Federals until thirty out of the forty men in his company were killed or wounded. General Jones's two brigades had done all they could against the well-placed Federals. Had Drayton's brigade attacked the Federal flank and rear in conjunction with Anderson and Benning, the attack would have rolled up the Federal line as Jones had planned. One Southern officer related, "Drayton's conduct is severely criticized by all who know anything of the officer." Although the attack failed to break the lines, the Southerners maintained a furious musketry from the cover of the woods.[45]

Farther south on Sudley Road, the situation changed quickly in favor of the Confederates. Stribling's and Eshleman's advancing batteries under Rosser attained a commanding position on the extreme left of the Federal line. From there, the Confederate gunners enfiladed the Federals, who were

trying to hold Sudley Road and Henry Hill. The fire of these batteries ultimately broke the extreme left flank of the Federal battle line, relieving the
pressure on the Confederate infantry. And just as these batteries made it hot
for the Federal infantry holding the left flank, Maj. Gen. Richard H. Anderson's fresh Confederate division crested Chinn Ridge and moved toward the
battle along Sudley Road.

Richard Heron Anderson, a South Carolina planter, had graduated
from West Point with Longstreet and had served in the war with Mexico and
on the frontier in the 2nd U.S. Dragoons. "General Dick Anderson was as
pleasant a commander to serve under as could be wished, and was a sturdy
and reliable fighter," noted a prominent Confederate officer. General Lee
had personally held Anderson's division in reserve until Lee was sure that
the threat to Jackson's weary troops had subsided. Lee's decision, prudent
as it may have been, contributed to his failure to destroy Pope's army. At the
outset of Longstreet's attack, Anderson's troops were posted north of the
Warrenton Turnpike. It was almost five o'clock before they finally advanced.
Passing to the south side of the turnpike, they double-quicked across the
farmland on the north side of the pike where Hood's men had initiated
their attack over an hour earlier. Anderson had deployed his division in two
lines of battle. Brig. Gen. Ambrose R. "Rans" Wright's brigade of Georgians
and Alabamans formed the left of Anderson's front line. When they first
advanced, Wright's left flank rested upon the Warrenton Turnpike, while
Brig. Gen. William Mahone posted his Virginians on Wright's southern or
right flank. Brig. Gen. Lewis A. Armistead's Virginia Brigade formed Anderson's Reserves, posted in line of battle directly behind the center of the
front line.[46]

Anderson's division followed the path of Hood's Texans, marching
through the fields strewn with dead and wounded Zouaves, and crossing
Young's Branch. Climbing out of the ravine, Mahone's Virginians came face
to face with Kerns's abandoned guns, the ground about them littered with
dead and wounded Pennsylvanians. As Anderson's men ascended the hill,
Sigel's gunners on Dogan Ridge caught sight of the fresh Confederates and
opened a deadly enfilading fire on them.

After passing over Chinn Ridge, Anderson's division marched up in line of battle under a heavy fire of artillery from the Federal batteries on Henry Hill, and never faltered. Wright's brigade made first contact with the enemy. Wright was a thirty-six-year-old lawyer who had started the war as a private in the Georgia Militia and soon was promoted to colonel of the 3rd Georgia Infantry. His brigade marched up behind D. R. Jones's engaged division and entered the combat in front of Chapman's Regulars as Wright's men relieved Colonel Anderson's brigade on the firing line. As Wright's brigade approached the woods west of Sudley Road, General Toombs galloped up and encouraged the Georgians in the most energetic terms. When the brigade entered the woods and approached Chapman's Regulars, numerous Confederates retired through Wright's battle line and warned the attacking Georgians not to fire, for there were more Confederate troops in front. Having dropped their guard as a result of the warning, the Wright's soldiers were stunned when Chapman's Regulars greeted the Southerners with "a destructive fire of musketry." Quickly recovering, Wright's Georgians and Alabamans charged through the woods, firing as they went. Above the din of battle, the Georgians heard the Chapman's officers crying out, "Fire! Fire low, boys!"[47]

At the same time, wiry Will Mahone's Virginians slid into position on Wright's left flank. At first, they encountered virtually no direct opposition but soon received an enfilading fire from the Federal batteries on Henry Hill to their left. As the Virginians closed in on Sudley Road, the 83rd New York and the 17th U.S. on the left of the Federal line opened fire. The fusillade temporarily stalled the Virginians' forward progress, but Mahone quickly shifted his brigade farther south so that it would extend beyond the Federal left flank. By now, Rosser had deployed a section of Eshleman's Washington Artillery just east of Sudley Road and only a few hundred yards distant from the Federal left. The Louisiana gunners sent two rounds of canister into the uncovered left flank of the 83rd New York. Rocked by the dual blasts of canister, the 83rd New York came unhinged and headed for the rear, shouting, "It is too hot!" as they passed the Regulars.[48]

The 83rd New York's retreat in turn exposed Chapman's left flank to Eshleman's guns and Mahone's Virginians. Stribling's battery soon rolled

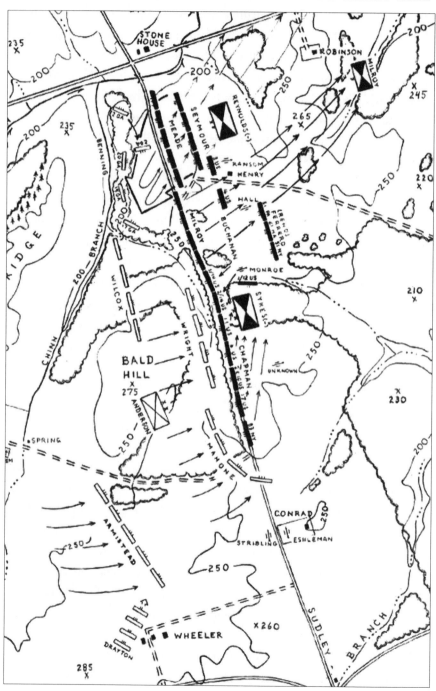

John C. McAnaw

into position near Eshleman and increased the Confederate artillery fire directed at the now shaky Union left flank. Finding the Regulars in a tenuous position, with Wright's Georgians and Alabamans pressing against his front and Mahone's Virginians moving against the Regulars' left flank, Chapman passed the word along his battle line to fall back. The withdrawal went smoothly until the 83rd New York crashed through the ranks of the 17th U.S., but by the time the Regulars had passed through the woods and entered the fields atop Henry Hill, order had been restored. Passing a rail fence set afire by Rebel artillery, Mahone's Virginians crossed to the east side of Sudley Road, when a Federal Minié ball knocked Mahone out of the battle, causing a temporary halt of the advance that likely allowed Chapman to get away without additional damage to his brigade. Command of Mahone's brigade devolved upon Col. David Weisiger of the 12th Virginia Infantry. Weisiger quickly oriented himself to the situation and sorted it out by wheeling the Virginians to the left and entering the woods on the southern edge of Henry Hill.

When Chapman's Regulars withdrew, Wright's brigade directed its efforts against Milroy. His "Boys," as he referred to them, "began to show signs of mistrust and started by two's and three's to leave the line." The fire from Wright's brigade and other Confederates in the woods in front had become overwhelming, and their ammunition had run out entirely. Milroy had no other choice but to order them to the rear and dispatch an aide to request reinforcements from General McDowell. The aide soon returned, telling Milroy that McDowell had refused to send help. The irate Hoosier "flew" rapidly to Henry Hill and found McDowell "sitting calmly on his horse amidst his numerous staff and body guard." Milroy appealed to McDowell "in the most energetic manner for a brigade, telling him that the crises [sic] of the battle and of the nation was at hand and not a moment was to be lost." Taken aback by Milroy's frenzied manner, McDowell coldly replied that "he was not bound to help everybody and that he was not going to help General Sigel." Milroy informed McDowell that he was not fighting with Sigel but with troops from "half a dozen different brigades." Milroy added, "All I know is that we are trying hard to whip the rebels." McDowell then asked Milroy if Brigadier General Meade were fighting with Meade's Pennsylvania Reserves in the road cut. Milroy didn't know, but one of McDowell's aides answered positively. With that McDowell said he "would send [Meade] help for he was a good fellow," and ordered Porter to reinforce Meade. Porter passed the order to Sykes, who then sent Buchanan's brigade to Meade's aid.[49]

Robert Huston Milroy believed that he was fighting the pivotal battle for the preservation of the United States. Afterward he wrote, "I felt that the crisis of the nation was on hand, and that the happiness of unborn millions and the progress of the world depended upon our success." Yet Milroy's enraged manner only prompted those who saw him to inquire, "Who is that rushing about so wildly and what does he want?" Porter concluded that Milroy was "demented." Buchanan considered the Hoosier "a crazy man." Although Milroy meant well, McDowell could not responsibly place troops in the hands of an officer whose emotions seemed to have overtaken his rationality. After completing his obligation to inform McDowell of the situation along Sudley Road, Milroy should have returned to his brigade, leaving command of the troops entering the battle to their designated commanders. Instead, Milroy remained on Henry Hill attempting to hijack commands as they entered the battle. Although McDowell had treated Milroy curtly, the major general did ultimately recognize the seriousness of the situation and did send Buchanan forward with three Regular battalions.

Buchanan led a battalion of the 12th U.S. and two from the 14th U.S. toward the besieged Federal line in the Sudley Road cut. These Regulars went into the position formerly occupied by Chapman's right and Milroy's left. Capt. Matthew M. Blunt's battalion of the 12th U.S. anchored Buchanan's left flank, facing southward toward the woods to confront Mahone's Virginians. Capt. David B. McKibbin's and Capt. John D. O'Connell's battalions of the 14th U.S. occupied the road where Milroy's right flank had been previously stationed. The woods in their front limited their visibility and sheltered Wright's Georgians there.

As soon as Buchanan started forward with the 12th and 14th U.S., Milroy galloped over to Buchanan's two remaining battalions, the 3rd and 4th U.S. Infantry. The fervid Hoosier darted out in front of the Regulars and "told the boys to come on." Accustomed to tight-lipped Regular Army officers, they were surprised by Milroy's spirit and zeal. The men in the ranks gave "three cheers" and followed him on the double-quick. Milroy led them forward and deployed the Regulars upon the embankment behind the road cut in rear of Meade's brigade. With the 3rd U.S. on the right and 4th U.S. on the left, these battalions fired six volleys, silencing the Confederates in the woods in front of Reynolds. The Confederates now ceased in their direct attacks on Reynolds's sector of the battle line and henceforth concentrated their final efforts against the extreme Federal left.[50]

As Buchanan completed posting the 12th and 14th U.S., he looked over to his right and saw Milroy shouting orders to the 3rd and 4th U.S., which Buchanan had left in the rear. Surprised to see that they had advanced, Buchanan galloped over to confront Milroy, sternly informing him, "Those battalions belong to my brigade of Regulars, and that I could not consent to any interference with my command." Milroy replied, "I did not know they were your men, did not wish to interfere with you, and I only wanted to place them in the best position." Buchanan responded that placing these battalions was his responsibility and that he needed no assistance with his duties. With that, Milroy rode to the rear in search of more troops to lead. For his part, Buchanan recognized that the real threat was coming from R. H. Anderson's division against the Federal left and shifted the 3rd and 4th U.S. farther south on the right flank of Captain O'Connell's battalion of the 14th U.S. As the Regulars filed to the left, Reynolds's Pennsylvania Reserves withdrew to the right and then marched to the rear in a withdrawal that seems to have been poorly coordinated.[51]

Capt. John D. "Paddy" O'Connell had graduated from West Point in 1852. He had helped raise and train the newly formed 14th U.S. Infantry in 1861. The new unit had enrolled a large foreign-born contingent, including many Irishmen, Austrians, and Germans. Cpl. Peter Petroff and his nephew, for example, had come from Saint Petersburg, Russia, to fight in the great American Rebellion. By 1862 O'Connell had melded this "melting pot" unit into one of the U.S. Regular Army's premier units. In turn, the soldiers of the 14th U.S. admired and respected O'Connell. One remembered, "With him, the interest of the men came first, the officers second and his own last."[52]

O'Connell had already been wounded that day when repulsing a Confederate counterattack during Porter's retreat. Now occupying Sudley Road,
he saw what he thought was a U.S. flag moving in the woods west of the road
and rode out to identify the troops bearing it. He found his answer when
Rebel bullets killed his horse and struck his knee. O'Connell limped back to
his battalion, ordered the men to fire, and turned command over to Capt.
Harvey Brown. Certain that no friends were in front, the 14th U.S. delivered
four volleys into Wright's brigade. To O'Connell's left, McKibbin's battalion
added several rounds of its own, checking the Georgians' progress. Yet the
Regulars sensed that Confederates were moving up in force on their left
flank. McKibbin dispatched his sergeant major and two other men to recon-
noiter the situation south of their position. They soon ran back to McKibbin
and informed him that the Confederates, Mahone's Virginians, followed by
Brig. Gen. Lewis A. Armistead's and Drayton's brigades, were moving up in
large numbers and flanking the Federal position. McKibbin changed front
to meet the new threat. On McKibbin's left, Captain Blunt's 12th U.S. fired
blindly into the woods east of Sudley Road. Although Blunt could not see
into the dark woods, the volleys of the 12th U.S. struck Weisiger's Virginians
with deadly effect, forcing them to halt their advance and lie down on the
slope of Henry Hill.

As daylight waned, the Confederates intended to make one last effort to
crush Pope's left flank. R. H. Anderson ordered Armistead's brigade of Virginians to support Mahone's brigade. Armistead's Confederates crossed to
the east side of the Sudley Road and moved into position on Mahone's right
flank. Once Armistead arrived on the Federal flank at the southern end of
Henry Hill, his brigade lay down on the hillside and contributed nothing to
the Confederate offensive. On the other end of Anderson's battle line, Brig.
Gen. Cadmus Wilcox's Alabama finally arrived and relieved Wright's bloodied Georgians as the Regulars' began to withdraw under increasing Confederate pressure. Mahone's Virginians continued to fire sporadically into the
12th U.S. on Buchanan's left flank, but did not immediately advance. Captain Blunt realized that the 12th U.S. was flanked on the left and ordered
a withdrawal. The 12th's withdrawal exposed the left flank of the 14th U.S.

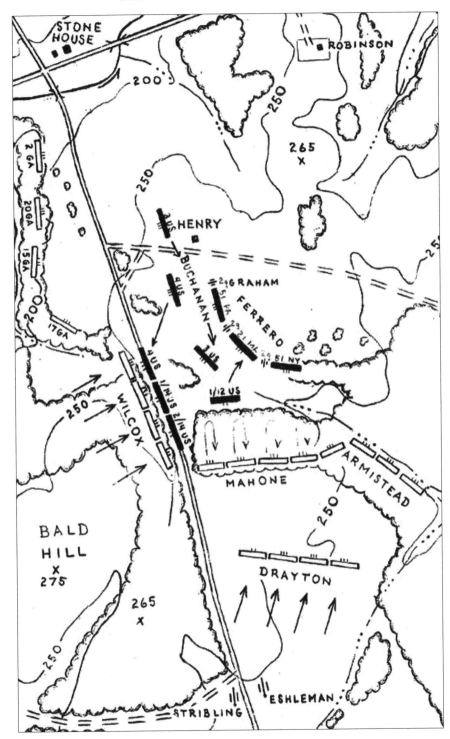

John C. McAnaw

to an enfilading fire from Mahone's Virginians at the same time Wilcox's Alabamans struck the front. Consequently, the entire 14th U.S. pulled out of Sudley Road and joined the 12th U.S. in retreat.

Just before the 12th U.S. began its retreat, the 3rd and 4th U.S. completed their leftward shift. The 4th U.S. took position in Sudley Road on the right flank of the 14th U.S. The 3rd remained on the embankment behind the road to the right and rear of the 4th. These two battalions held their fire until Wilcox's Alabamans had approached to within thirty yards. Then the 3rd U.S. loosed three volleys and the men of the 4th triggered four rounds each before the Alabamans could respond with a volley of their own. By the time the Regulars stopped firing, the 14th U.S. had withdrawn with the 12th U.S. and formed a second line of battle behind the 3rd and 4th U.S.— a textbook withdrawal that few units outside the Regular Army could have coordinated so well.

With R. H. Anderson's overwhelming Confederate force on his left flank, Buchanan gave the order to withdraw at seven o'clock, three hours after Longstreet's attack began. Wilcox's Alabamans fired into the Regulars as they retreated. Nevertheless, after proceeding only thirty yards in retreat, the 3rd and 4th U.S. halted, faced about, and gave the Alabamans another volley that kept them at bay. Then, the Regulars turned around and continued their withdrawal. The Regulars had only covered sixty yards more when the Confederate fire again grew in severity. Once again the 3rd and 4th U.S. halted, turned around, and fired two volleys into the Alabamans. Once it was ascertained that the Confederates were no longer following, Buchanan ordered the brigade to return to its original position near the burned-out house on Henry Hill. As the Regulars moved across the plateau, General McDowell rode up and taking off his hat shouted: "God Bless you, Regulars! You've saved the army! You shall not be forgotten! God bless you, everyone!" Flattered, the U.S. Army soldiers cheered him in return, for until now they had not "realized the value of the work they had done in the country lane." McDowell's presence on the front lines did not go unnoticed either.[53]

Although the Regulars were marching away, McDowell had made accommodations to cover their retreat. Maj. Gen. Jesse Reno led Col. Edward

Ferrero's small brigade into position on Henry Hill to cover the retreat. Although Pope, McDowell, and Porter had thwarted the Confederate effort to cut off the Army of Virginia at its line of retreat over Bull Run Bridge, the opportunity remained to disrupt the otherwise orderly withdrawal. The Southerners had plenty of troops on hand to finish the job, but lacked leadership on the scene. Drayton's and Armistead's brigades had yet to fire a shot. Weisiger's Virginians had suffered lightly compared to the other Confederate brigades that had assaulted Sudley Road, while Wilcox's Alabamans had endured even less. Yet no Confederate officer with proper rank and authority was present to coordinate an all-out push against Henry Hill. Maj. Gen. Jeb Stuart encouraged Armistead to attack, but the infantryman demurred. Instead, several uncoordinated attacks struck the Union rear guard atop the hill.

As Reno led Ferrero's brigade into position on Henry Hill, the now-advanced Confederate batteries shelled the marching Federals as the clock passed seven. A soldier of the 21st Massachusetts declared, "Such cannonading I have never before heard. The balls, shells and railroad iron came over our heads like rain." Reno deployed his troops in a semicircle that conformed to the southern edge of the Henry Hill plateau. The 51st New York deployed on Ferrero's left, with its flank resting upon a small stream. The 21st Massachusetts deployed in the center of the brigade, while Col. John Hartranft's 51st Pennylvania anchored the right. Reno posted the smooth-bored Napoleons of Capt. William M. Graham's Battery K, 1st U.S. Artillery, on the crest of the hill behind the infantry. As was rapidly becoming the norm on Henry Hill, the "irrepressible" General Milroy dashed up and attempted to hijack command of Ferrero's brigade, riding along the battle line and "shouting like a crazy man." Reno quickly ended Milroy's antics, firmly ordering the wild-eyed Hoosier "not to interfere further in the management of the brigade." With that threat to order eliminated, Reno calmly instructed his soldiers to lie down and maintain absolute silence. Then Reno, a native-born Virginian, posted himself in the center of his line and waited for the Rebels to make their next move.[54]

By now the sun had settled in behind the Bull Run Mountains to the west and darkness began to engulf the battlefield. Reno's men suddenly heard "a confused hum and the rush of many feet" as the Confederates in their front, elements of Mahone's and Wilcox's brigades, advanced out of the woods to the south and southwest and charged up Henry Hill. Reno commanded the men to stand up, and "give them about ten rounds, boys, fire!" Graham's battery fired in unison with the infantry, and the results were devastating. Before Ferrero's troops could get "warmed up," the firing died down and quiet reigned for thirty minutes, except for the groans and cries of the wounded Rebels in front.[55]

During the lull, Captain Graham repositioned his guns on line with Reno's infantry, deploying in the intervals between the regiments. The quiet ended when elements of Drayton's brigade crawled up along the banks of a creek off in the low ground to the left of the 51st New York and opened fire. The Georgians and South Carolinians quickly rolled up the New Yorkers' flank and forced them to retreat, but Reno's men rose to meet the occasion.[56]

The New Yorkers fell back a short distance, but changed front and opened fire. At the same time, the 21st Massachusetts quickly changed front to the left and delivered a volley into the darkness in the direction of the Confederates. Captain Graham rushed two guns into position on the left flank of the 51st New York, and the combined fire of the big guns and the infantry ended the Confederate threat. The Confederates probed Reno's position once more with a skirmish line, but the Yankees responded with a volley to let the Southerners know "we were still there." Aside from artillery firing, the combat had ended. At nine o'clock, Reno gave the order, and his command marched away, leaving Henry Hill to the Confederates.[57]

Although the fighting had gone against the U.S. Army of Virginia, the precise outcome was not yet readily apparent to many in both Union and Confederate armies. Confederate generals Wright and Toombs "did not know how complete our victory had been and supposed that the enemy would attack us early in the morning." Franz Sigel was furious when he learned that the army was abandoning the field. George Sykes believed that the line could have been held if his and Reynolds's commands had been "properly sustained." The ubiquitous General Milroy felt certain that Pope would renew "the great, glorious drama of the war" in the morning. As the

Hoosier searched for his brigade in the darkness, he could not find them or any other troops near the front. Mystified, he rode on toward Bull Run in "painful, bewildering doubt." Then he found Sigel, who told him that the army was falling back to Centreville. This news hit Milroy with "agonizing surprise," for in his mind the Union forces should have renewed the fighting on the next morning where they left on that evening.[58]

The news of the retreat should not have surprised anyone. The Army of Virginia had narrowly avoided disaster. As it was, its units were scattered, and the men had lost confidence in their commanders. Intrigue plagued the high command. Retreat was their only realistic option under the circumstances. When his army reached the defenses of Washington after retreating through northern Virginia, Maj. Gen. George B. McClellan once again took command, and Pope's forces became part of the Army of the Potomac. The change met with the hearty approbation of the fighting men. Ephraim Bisel of the 10th U.S. Infantry, which had fought in Sudley Road, wrote, "I never saw men rejoice so much in my life as when McClellan met us when we were coming towards Washington; some literally wept for joy."[59]

Six

"WE ARE FRIENDS NOW"

THE CESSATION OF COMBAT on the fields of Manassas brought relief to the soldiers of both armies. The Army of Virginia retreated to Centreville, where most of the men lay down for some well-deserved sleep. A Massachusetts soldier of Ferrero's brigade wrote, "Our regt. covered the retreat of our army to Centreville; and when I stopped that night, I sank down in the mud asking only to be let alone. I shall never forget that march. So full of grief and pain and shame."[1]

When the firing finally ceased, those who were still standing saw the destruction that their labor had produced. Nearly ten thousand Federals and eight thousand Confederates lay scattered across the fields and forests of Manassas battlefield, many of them slowly dying far from family and friends. The "dismal moans and heart rending cries of the wounded and dying" prevented many survivors from sleeping that night. In addition to the human loss, "every conceivable article pertaining to an army" littered the ground. One Confederate surveyed the human carnage strewn about Chinn Ridge, and exclaimed, "Oh, the horrid scenes around us! Brains, fractured skulls, broken arms and legs, and the human form mangled in every conceivable and inconceivable manner."[2]

As darkness fell, the victorious Confederates gathered up their wounded and a few fortunate Union wounded. Most of them eventually ended up inside and around the Chinn House and its outbuildings. As the combat moved away from Hazel Plain, Cpl. George W. Wise of the 17th Virginia escorted a Union prisoner to the rear. Passing a ravine near the house, Wise found his fallen commander, Lt. Col. Morton Marye, lying on a stretcher there being tended by two comrades. Because Marye was a large man, the two soldiers with him lacked the strength to carry him to the house. Wise and his prisoner grabbed one end of the stretcher and assisted in carrying the Virginian to the field hospital.

At the field hospital, Col. Montgomery Corse, who had been slightly wounded during the closing scenes of combat on Chinn Ridge, informed Marye that the doctors must amputate his leg in order to save his life. The news distressed Marye, of course, but Corse reminded him of their Virginians' capture of Leppien's battery and several battle flags, telling Marye, "Colonel, when they stick the knife in, you must not flinch, for this is the happiest day of the 1st brigade." Marye survived the removal of his leg and went on to become the auditor of public accounts for the Commonwealth of Virginia, living until 1910.[3]

Soldiers of the 1st South Carolina of Jenkins's brigade carried the mortally wounded Colonel Glover to the Chinn House. They were deeply attached to the highly regarded Glover, for he had always looked out for their well-being. Even as he lay dying in the field hospital, he still put his men's needs ahead of his own. Pointing to his boots lying on the ground, Glover turned to a comrade and feebly muttered, "Give them to one of my barefooted soldiers."[4]

As night came on, many individual Confederate soldiers scoured the field for missing comrades, hoping they would not turn up dead. Capt. D. R. McCallum of the 23rd South Carolina walked the battlefield, guided by torchlight, searching for the dead and wounded men from his company alongside similar parties from every Confederate regiment.

The wounded Federals strewn across Chinn Ridge received little aid and comfort that night. Those who could still walk struggled to the Chinn House as circumstances permitted. One of them, Erskine Carson of the 73rd Ohio, had been wounded in the left leg and hobbled through the Chinn orchard until he reached the woodshed, where he bedded down for the night. To make matters worse, some Confederate stragglers stole Carson's pocket watch and blanket. Carson recalled the night as being one of horror:

> Saturday night was a gloomy night, for all through the night there came the groaning and crying of men who were undergoing operations in the stone [Chinn] house that can never be effaced from my memory. During the night a Rebel soldier crawled up alongside of me, shot through both legs and it was piteous to hear him cry from the suffering his wounds caused him.[5]

Carson lay on the field for several days before anyone tended his wounds. On Sunday night, he experienced severe abdominal pains that distressed him even more than his leg wound. A Georgian belonging to the ambulance corps stopped to talk with him. Learning of the Ohioan's suffering, the "kind hearted" Georgian administered a healthy dose of laudanum, which provided Carson "immediate relief." The two enemies established a rapport and traded addresses, hoping to meet again. On Monday Carson, along with many of the Federal wounded, received a parole and was taken to the Fairfax County Courthouse in an ambulance; his military service had ended. Two years later in Ohio, Carson received a letter from the Georgian, who had been taken prisoner at Gettysburg. The Georgian had taken the oath of allegiance and now needed a place to go to in the North. Carson arranged a job for the Georgian on the Marietta and Cincinnati Railroad, allowing him to begin a new chapter of his life in Ohio.[6]

Pvt. W. R. Houghton of the 2nd Georgia had been shot through his right hand by a Minié ball while battling Koltes's brigade on Chinn Ridge. He remained on the field while the combat had raged, using a dead Confederate to shield himself from the deadly gunfire. As the combat faded, a sense of loneliness came over Houghton; he felt like "a broken wheel, a useless machine, with no companions and no food." Wandering about the battlefield in search of his comrades, Private Houghton was unable to find anyone in the dark of night, so he finally ended up sleeping at the Chinn House.

The next morning he "walked among the numerous dead who covered the fields. . . . Out of sheer loneliness and wretchedness," he sat down and talked to a group of wounded Federals and made quick friends with a captain from Pennsylvania. After the war Houghton recalled their meeting:

> His ankle was shattered, but he had hands, coffee and rations. I brought wood and water; he made a fire and some very good coffee. He shared the contents of his haversack with me, and under the influence of a good meal, our spirits revived. He pressed me to visit him or call on him for any favor, and as good friends we parted, he in an ambulance train under flag of truce for Washington, and I for a weary walk to Culpeper, a hospital experience, and a sixty days furlough. I trust that the courteous Pennsylvanian, at once my enemy, host and friend, yet lives in prosperity.[7]

Sam Lowry of the 17th South Carolina lay on Chinn Ridge writhing in pain from a leg wound, with wounded men lying all around him. Another soldier sat down beside Lowry, exclaiming, "We are friends now if we have been enemies." The South Carolinian did not understand the man, being too focused on examining his wounded leg. Then he noticed the man's blue uniform and inquired what regiment he belonged to. He replied, "I belong to the 25th Ohio," and added, "I am tired of this d—d war and won't fight anymore." Lowry took his gun and turned him over to some passing Confederates. Lowry then limped to the Chinn House, where he met a comrade who bound his wound and gave him an oilcloth and blanket. Lowry staggered into the cellar of the Chinn House, where he spent the night pouring cold water on his wound. A doctor from a Virginia regiment then bandaged Lowry's leg, leaving him feeling "very comfortable," a feeling few wounded knew that night on Chinn Ridge.[8]

On Bald Hill Capt. C. R. Jennings of the 26th New York lay helplessly wounded until nine o'clock that night. Although the Southerners overran his position soon after he fell, they treated him with "the greatest kindness." Many halted to provide Jennings a much-needed drink of water. At length, a Captain Canty from Jenkins's South Carolina brigade found Jennings lying on the field and ordered some of his men to carry the wounded New Yorker to the crowded Chinn House. There, Confederate surgeons treated Jennings as they would have cared for a fellow Southerner and made no exceptions because he was a Federal. The whole experience prompted Jennings to write, "I must say that the Southerner is a brave, gentle and magnanimous enemy."[9]

In the Confederate ranks, the men took heart of their victory and wrote home to tell loved ones they had survived another battle. The 2nd Georgia's Theodore Fogle penned, "Oh Mother, a merciful God has wonderfully preserved me. Men were shot down all around me, balls and missiles of death of every kind whistled by, but I never got a scratch."[10]

While some tended to the needs of the wounded, other Confederates plied the battlefield for booty from dead Federals. A good-sized soldier of the 5th Texas sought a pair of trousers large enough to fit him properly. Although the thought of robbing the dead bothered the superstitious Texan, he finally mustered the courage to undertake his search around midnight. He wandered the battlefield in awe of the dead and wounded around him, fully expecting to encounter a ghost. At last he came upon a large Federal rolled up in an oilcloth. The Texan began unbuckling the man's trousers, when the supposedly dead Yankee shot up to a sitting position and exclaimed, "Great God alive, man! Don't rob me before I am dead, if you please!" The terrified Texan "sprang twenty feet at one bound" but quickly regained his composure, figuring that "no ghost would speak so sensibly." The Texan instantly apologized, adding, "Please pardon me and let me know what I can do to make amends for my rudeness." The wounded Federal asked for water, and the Texan gave up his canteen and ended his search for trousers.[11]

After the battle, Mrs. William Mahone received notice of her bony little husband's wounding and grew worried for his well-being. Attempting to alleviate her fears, the messenger told Mrs. Mahone that her husband had received only a flesh wound. The general's wife became even more worried and sharply retorted, "You are deceiving me, for if a bullet struck him, it must have hit a bone." Will Mahone would survive his wound and go on to become an efficient division commander during the war's last year, playing a key role in the combats around Petersburg.[12]

For all of the wounded after the Second Battle of Manassas, thousands more lay dead on the battlefield. The slain of both sides were initially interred on the battlefield. Families of wealthy and influential officers and men later retrieved the remains of their fallen heroes and had them reburied in their hometowns. After the war, many of the Confederate dead were gathered and reburied in the Groveton Confederate Cemetery; all but a few were buried as unknown soldiers in unmarked graves. Most of the Federal dead were reinterred in Arlington National Cemetery during the years immediately following the war. Undoubtedly, some Union and Confederate soldiers lie buried in unmarked graves throughout the woods and fields of Manassas National Battlefield.

For the Union soldiers, the defeat at the Second Battle of Manassas weighed heavily on their minds in the days and weeks that followed. Morale plummeted as the men realized that their great losses would not have been necessary had Pope and company heeded the multiple warnings of Longstreet's presence. One dying officer declared himself "a victim of Pope's imbecility and McDowell's treason." Jesse Bowsher and August Wormley of the 55th Ohio summed up the feelings of many soldiers when they wrote home, "If you have a spare drink, send it down this way, as we have had none for a long time. If you can't send it, drink and remember us."[13]

For the Union army, McDowell's removal of Reynolds's division from Chinn Ridge after Porter's repulse opened the door to disaster. Colonel McLean firmly believed that "if Reynolds's division had remained with my brigade, we could have successfully held the hill." McLean felt that McDowell had expected the Ohio Brigade "to do the work of an army corps." The plucky Ohioan termed McDowell's actions "the great mistake." A soldier from the 10th U.S. Infantry of Sykes's division declared, "I never want to see McDowell on the field again as a commander." His fervent wish was fulfilled.[14]

For Gen. John Pope, the end came quickly. As the Army of Virginia marched into the defenses of Washington, McClellan took them under his command, and Pope returned to Illinois. Addressing a crowd that had gathered beneath his balcony in Chicago, Pope announced,

My friends, I am glad to see you to-night. I am glad to be back to breathe again the pure air of the State of Illinois. It has been for many years my home, and I am glad to return to it. God Almighty only knows how sorry I am I ever left it.[15]

His reputation in the army was shattered. Brig. Gen. Alpheus S. Williams of Banks's Corps wrote,

More insolence, superciliousness, ignorance, and pretentiousness were never combined in one man. It can with truth be said of him that he had not a friend in his command from the smallest drummer boy to the highest general officer. All hated him.[16]

In spite of the defeat, most Union soldiers remained devoted to the cause of restoring the United States as one nation. A soldier of the 25th Ohio wrote,

The boys are still willing to follow Lee and Jackson even to the ends of the earth, for this great rebellion must be put down, lest it cost the lives of us all. The Stars and Stripes that our forefathers fought to preserve must still wave triumphant over our land, cost what it may.[17]

This attitude ultimately carried the Union on to victory.

Seven

UNION DISASTER AVERTED

AFTER THE SOUTHERN VICTORY at the Second Battle of Manassas, Confederate brigadier general W. Dorsey Pender declared, "There was never such a campaign, not even by Napoleon." Indeed, Gen. Robert E. Lee's Army of Northern Virginia had arguably achieved its greatest victory of the war, inflicting a 21 percent casualty rate on Pope while losing only 16 percent of its troops. At Chancellorsville, Lee's other great victory, he lost 25 percent of his men while inflicting only 15 percent losses on the Army of the Potomac. Chancellorsville repulsed a Union offensive in Virginia and did not lead to any immediate follow-up action, whereas Second Manassas opened the door for the immediate Confederate invasion of Maryland and the resulting battle along the banks of Antietam Creek. In the end, however, Lee did not come close to threatening the continued functional existence of the Army of the Potomac. Jackson soundly whipped one of the smaller Union corps, but the ongoing effectiveness of the Federal army was never at risk the way it was on August 30, 1862.[1]

Although Second Manassas was a resounding Confederate victory, it fell far short of reaching its potential—the effective destruction of Pope's Army of Virginia as a cohesive fighting force. Never before or after would Lee have such a realistic opportunity to achieve the Napoleonic goal of defeating an opponent so badly that his army ceased being an effective fighting force. At

Second Manassas, that opportunity clearly existed and remained a very real possibility until the stiff resistance of McLean's Ohioans on Chinn Ridge forcibly shattered the momentum of Longstreet's attack.

Earlier that summer, Lee had seen his army bleed profusely in the Seven Days Battles in front of Richmond. Despite that Confederate victory, the Federal army had escaped intact and remained a threat to be dealt with. Lee believed that the quickest way to win the war was to cripple his opponent's army and hoped to achieve such a strategic victory at Second Manassas. When the time to strike arrived, his "Old War Horse," Longstreet, rose to the occasion and attacked before receiving Lee's orders. Together, Lee and Longstreet would engineer one of the greatest Confederate victories of the war, yet they had hoped to accomplish more than they actually did.

Lee and Longstreet intended their hastily launched counterpunch to be a massive effort, with Henry Hill and its commanding position over the crossings of Young's Branch as its objective. Yet the Texas Brigade quickly outdistanced its supporting lines, which Longstreet saw. He attempted to rectify the situation, but the Texans had already gone too far. Although they achieved a stunning success at the tactical level, the Texans' lightning-quick advance severely disrupted the timing of Longstreet's attack. By the time Hood's supporting cast arrived, most of the Texas Brigade had fallen back, and the attack degenerated into an uncoordinated assault on Chinn Ridge. After routing the Pennsylvania Reserves, Hood's brigade should have regrouped and engaged McLean's Ohioans in a holding action. Then Evans and Kemper could have swept in and crushed McLean's flank at the first onset. Longstreet's attack could have next surged down Chinn Ridge toward Henry Hill, with all of his units intact and working in unison. Instead, Chinn Ridge turned into a Confederate bloodbath.

The rapid advance of Hood's men also made it difficult for Longstreet's orders to be carried out, as Hood's men were to be the guide upon which the rest of Longstreet's wing would attack. After explaining to Hood his objective, Longstreet directed Kemper to guide his advance on Hood's right flank. In turn, D. R. Jones aligned his division's course on Kemper's movements. Wherever Hood went, the others would follow—if they could find him, a potentially difficult task given the Texans' rapid advance.

A confusing command structure in the Evans/Hood division also contributed to the lack of coordination in the attack. Brigadier General "Shanks" Evans officially commanded a division composed of his own, Law's, and Hood's brigades. Yet Hood retained direct command of his own and Law's brigades, and Longstreet appeared to have essentially bypassed Evans and dealt with Hood. This resulted in poor coordination between the Texas Brigade and Evans's South Carolinians in the second line of battle. Proper cooperation between the Texans and Carolinians could have ended McLean's stand at its inception. Although Hood commanded a two-brigade division, he further complicated matters by failing to designate a capable brigade commander in his absence from the brigade, although he had two fine candidates in Colonel Wofford of the 18th Georgia and Colonel Robertson of the 5th Texas. Instead, Hood placed his adjutant-general, Capt. W. H. Sellers, in command of the Texas Brigade. In Hood's absence, Captain Sellers's accomplishments included an attempt to halt the brigade as it moved on the Pennsylvania Reserves and ordering the 1st Texas back to Young's Branch as it attempted to move forward to support the brigade in front of Chinn Ridge.

Another factor to consider is the role of Brigadier General Evans. As a result of Longstreet bypassing him in the chain of command, Evans had little impact, positive or negative, on the battle's outcome and simply seemed to be along for the ride. Reflecting on Evans's behavior throughout the Second Manassas Campaign, Longstreet's acting adjutant-general Maj. Moxley Sorrel noted, "Evans was reputedly difficult to manage, and we found him so." Sorrel also claimed to have found Evans "under a tree" with his "Barrelita" full of whiskey during a skirmish at Rappahannock Station on August 23. In spite of Sorrel's criticism, Longstreet nevertheless included Evans on his list of those officers who "prominently distinguished themselves" in the Second Manassas Campaign. During the combat on August 30, a Texan recalled that Evans dashed up to Hood's brigade "on a gray charger" while most of the brigade was resting back along Young's Branch under orders from Captain Sellers. The South Carolinian "rallied himself," waved his hat, and "eulogized" the Texans, before leading his command "on to the fight in his usual way."

Evans's keen tactical eye could have made a difference in front of Chinn Ridge, but for an uncertain reason, he did not significantly factor into the battle's outcome.[2]

The lack of a brigade commander on the field with the Texas Brigade forced three of the regimental commanders to halt and hold a conference and jointly decide on what course of action should be taken in front of Chinn Ridge. Had Hood allowed the senior to command the brigade (as occurred at South Mountain and Antietam), Hood's brigade might have been able to launch a more coordinated effort against McLean's Ohioans. If all five of the brigade's regiments had hit Chinn Ridge together, McLean might have been swept from the heights in the first rush, even before Hood's support arrived. Hood's failure to appoint a competent commander for the Texas Brigade prevented it from accomplishing much more than it did and caused the separation of its regiments at the very time that close coordination was needed most. Most important, the lack of guidance for the Texas Brigade resulted in its premature removal from the battle and disrupted the overall timing of the offensive. It was so bad that the 1st Texas did not have an opportunity to engage in the infantry combat before Sellers halted its advance.

Also, in Hood's division Colonel Law's brigade did not contribute to the success of the initial attack, largely because that command was confronted by the powerful array of Union artillery posted on Dogan Ridge. When the attack commenced, Law advanced his brigade to Groveton, where it supported Southern artillery, while the Texas Brigade routed Warren's Zouaves and Hardin's Pennsylvania Reserves. Thirty minutes into the attack, Hood finally directed Law to move his brigade south of the Warrenton Turnpike to support the Texas Brigade. These orders arrived too late for Law to provide material support to the Texans early in the attack against the Ohioans deployed on Chinn Ridge. Had Hood moved Law at the outset of the attack into a better position to support the Texas Brigade, he would have provided a force to continue the momentum that the Texans gained when they steamrollered the Zouaves and Pennsylvania Reserves. Instead, the Confederates struck the Ohioans with determined but piecemeal attacks, forfeiting the momentum needed to destroy Pope's army.

Command structure problems also haunted Brig. Gen. Cadmus M. Wilcox, posted on Jackson's immediate right flank, north of the Warrenton Turnpike. Like Hood, Wilcox commanded his division as the senior brigade commander and retained command of his own brigade instead of appointing the senior colonel. This led to confusion in the later stages of Longstreet's attack. Early on in the counterattack, Longstreet ordered Wilcox to bring his division south of the Warrenton Turnpike to support Hood's attack. Since Wilcox interpreted these orders to mean that he should take only his own Alabama brigade to reinforce the attack, he left the two remaining brigades of his division north of the turnpike. Moreover, Wilcox was extremely slow in reaching the front, admittedly losing his way, and as a result he and his command played no meaningful role in the battle. Longstreet later blamed Wilcox for the Confederate failure to take Henry Hill, claiming that Wilcox had been ordered to bring his entire division south of the turnpike. However, both Wilcox and Brig. Gen. Winfield Scott Featherston agreed in their reports that the order was for Wilcox to bring only his brigade. Rather than an error on the part of Wilcox, a miscommunication on the part of some staff officer or courier contributed to the failure to implement Longstreet's instructions. Nevertheless, Wilcox did not command a division again until attrition placed him in that position later in the war.

Brig. Gen. James L. Kemper's inexperience as a division commander was reflected in his actions, or lack thereof, on the battlefield. Kemper's three brigades quickly began to act on their own volition, with Kemper exercising little, if any, coordination of their efforts. He allowed his brigades to be sucked into the maelstrom on Chinn Ridge, and it ultimately took a full division to accomplish what a single brigade might have, had the division's movements had been properly coordinated. His inexperience as a division commander clearly showed, but then again he was only a temporary commander serving for the wounded George Pickett. It must be said on Kemper's behalf that he pressed the attack and fought with his division until it could fight no more, but he showed very little tactical ability in maneuvering his command at Second Manassas.

While Hood and Kemper had erred on the aggressive side, Maj. Gen. Richard H. Anderson's timidity lost the final opportunity to break the Union battle line on Henry Hill and damage the Federal Army of Virginia. His division entered the battlefield as Jones's division battled the Federal defenders of Henry Hill. Anderson only needed to push Mahone's and Armistead's brigades forward. They were in the proper position but undertook no effective action. When Jeb Stuart found Armistead's brigade lying idle and anxiously urged the Virginians to launch a direct attack against the Union left flank that rested just in front of the Virginians, Armistead declined to advance in the darkness without the sanction of his commanding officer. With neither Anderson nor Longstreet on the scene, Stuart declined to order the Virginians forward. Capt. Robert M. Stribling, commanding the Fauquier Artillery serving with Stuart, noted Anderson's failure. He wrote in his report to Col. Edward P. Alexander:

> I have thought that had Anderson's Division followed the direction taken by the three batteries when advanced by General Stuart, that it could have fallen upon the flank of the enemy not far from the Lewis House and caused the abandonment of the Henry House Hill.[3]

Because Anderson's report on the Second Battle of Manassas has gone missing (which isn't uncommon for Confederate reports, as many were burned when Richmond fell in 1865), historians are left to speculate on why he did not press the attack against the Federals on Henry Hill. Although Anderson's actions are questionable, it is hard to formulate a valid analysis of his role in the battle without understanding his orders and possible reasons for his actions or lack thereof. Yet in hindsight, it is clear that had he aggressively pushed his entire division against the Union soldiers defending Henry Hill, the Army of Northern Virginia would have inflicted much more damage on Pope's army. Ironically, an attack that began with Hood's rapid and impetuous attack ended with R. H. Anderson's prudence and timidity in the face of opportunity.

Unlike Anderson, Brig. Gen. David R. Jones excelled and pressed the attack at every available opportunity that was presented to his division. When his command entered the combat, Jones quickly recognized that the key to success involved bypassing the Federal left flank on Chinn Ridge and seizing Henry Hill. He quickly set about to accomplish this objective, but Brig. Gen. Thomas Drayton's failure to advance promptly wasted an excellent opportunity for the Confederates to break the battle open for Longstreet.

Although some of Longstreet's division commanders failed to measure up, many of his brigade and regimental commanders excelled. Colonel Robertson and the 5th Texas contributed more to the success of Longstreet's attack than any other regiment. As Hood put it, the 5th Texas "slipped the bridle" in its explosive attack and by the time that the battle ended, the remnants of Robertson's regiment were fighting on the most advanced Confederate lines in front of Henry Hill. The success of the 5th Texas came at a tremendous cost. The regiment lost 260 killed or wounded, including its colonel, lieutenant colonel, and acting major. After the battle, the Texans counted twenty-seven bullet holes and three tears from shells in their battle flag. The aggressive actions of the 5th Texas at Second Manassas rank among the most impressive displays of fighting ability during the course of the Civil War. Additionally, Colonel Wofford's 18th Georgia and Lieutenant Colonel Gary's Hampton Legion also deserve mention for pressing forward and pressuring the Federals at a time when they had no brigade commander on the field. Col. Montgomery Corse and his Virginians turned the tide of battle on Chinn Ridge. Corse put his men into the fight and was key to the dispersal of the Federals from the ridge. Colonel "Rock" Benning's aggressiveness placed Chinn Ridge firmly in Confederate grasp and led the push toward Henry Hill.

One of the biggest mysteries at Second Manassas, at least in a superficial sense, was Stonewall Jackson's inability to quickly join the counterattack after the repulse of Porter's attack. After the war, Longstreet blamed the deceased Jackson for the failure of Lee's army to destroy Pope's force at Second Manassas. It is without doubt that Jackson's inaction allowed the Union forces to move from his front to confront Longstreet. When Longstreet launched his attack, Reynolds's division had already abandoned Chinn Ridge, leaving Warren's and McLean's brigades as the only Union defenders south of the Warrenton Turnpike. McDowell rushed Hardin's brigade back to the south side of the road, but Hood made short work of Warren's and Hardin's brigades, leaving only McLean to defend Chinn Ridge. All other Union troops who fought on Chinn Ridge, along Sudley Road, and on Henry Hill went into position in *response* to Longstreet's attack. They were able to do so because Jackson's wing on Longstreet's left flank north of the turnpike showed no threatening posture. Had Jackson at least demonstrated forcibly against the Federals in his front, many of the Union reinforcements that were rushed to Chinn Ridge and Henry Hill probably would not have been able to join the fighting south of the turnpike. When one remembers that Pope was fixated on Jackson, any substantial aggressive activity by Stonewall's wing would probably have prompted an overreaction on the part of Pope. However, by the time Jackson belatedly advanced, Longstreet's attack was nearly two hours old, and the optimal time for action on Jackson's part had long since passed.

While it is clear that more action on Jackson's part would have greatly aided Longstreet, one must examine the orders that "Old Jack" received from General Lee. At the outset of Longstreet's attack, Lee instructed Jackson, "General Longstreet is advancing; look out for and protect his left flank." If Lee wished for Jackson to advance with Longstreet, these orders clearly did not communicate that wish. In Civil War parlance, the word "protect" generally did not carry offensive or aggressive connotations.[4]

Given those orders, Jackson would have focused his movements on the troops nearest to his immediate right flank: Wilcox's division. As noted earlier, Wilcox failed to move his entire division to the south side of the Warrenton Turnpike as Longstreet had ordered. The two brigades of Wilcox that remained next to Jackson foundered and did not advance until the closing stages of the battle. From Jackson's perspective then, his troops appeared to have fulfilled Lee's orders to protect Longstreet's left flank because their movements were closely timed with the actions of Wilcox's two brigades. From Longstreet's perspective, Wilcox's division had been ordered away from Jackson's flank and should have been moving up behind Hood. But Wilcox misinterpreted his orders, and confusion reigned.

Yet, with both Lee and Longstreet observing the impact of the Union artillery in Jackson's front on the attack, it is highly unlikely that Lee would have permitted Jackson to remain inactive. According to Longstreet, Lee sent Jackson a second set of orders directly instructing him to attack the Federal batteries on Dogan Ridge. While Longstreet's memoirs have been a source of controversy, his claim that Lee sent Jackson these second orders is well within reason and even more, it is the obvious move Lee would want to make given the tactical situation.

Yet, before any wholesale blame can be cast on Jackson, the circumstances of his command must be examined within the context of the overall battle. When Longstreet attacked, much of Jackson's infantry was in no condition to launch an all-out assault north of the turnpike. His divisions and brigades had been shuffled along the battle line to meet the exigencies posed by Porter's attack, thus scattering Jackson's units and impairing command and control of the troops. When Porter's command retreated, several of Jackson's brigade commanders launched sporadic, local counterattacks against the Federals immediately in their own front. Without exception, these failed to achieve any noteworthy success beyond rounding up laggards from Porter's command owing to the well-posted Federal artillery and masses of infantry north of the turnpike. This thick array of Union firepower in front of Jackson no doubt impressed upon Stonewall that the Federals in his front were far from beaten and were in fact strongly positioned. As a result, any large-scale movement on Jackson's part would not be without risk. Another factor to consider is that a number of Jackson's units had expended their ammunition in repelling Porter, and it would take time to have them resupplied before any serious effort was made.

Nevertheless, Jackson should have created a large-scale diversion north of the turnpike. He should have used his artillery more effectively against the Federal batteries on Dogan Ridge. Although they would have been outgunned and would have suffered severely in the short term, they would have been attracting the Union gunners' attention away from Longstreet's infantry and forcing them to provide counterbattery fire instead of infantry support for the Union defenders. Jackson made no effective effort, and the Dogan Ridge batteries wreaked havoc in Longstreet's ranks. Jackson also had Col. H. B. Strong's relatively unscathed Louisiana brigade posted in reserve near Sudley Church. A diversion by Strong's brigade backed by Maj. Gen. Ambrose P. Hill's division, which had not been directly hit by Porter's attack, against Pope's extreme right flank might well have sent shock waves through the Union chain of command and paralyzed the movement of reinforcements to Chinn Ridge and Henry Hill. Such a move may have very well created a panic among the Federals with the specter of Confederates attacking both flanks of the Union army. Another factor to consider is that Longstreet's attack began so suddenly upon the repulse of Porter, that very little time existed for proper coordination of action with Jackson. Prior to Porter's repulse, Longstreet's assignment had been to conduct a reconnaissance in force, and "Old Pete" turned it into a full-blown counterattack even before General Lee ordered him to do so.

For the Union army, Maj. Gen. Irvin McDowell's removal of Reynolds's division from Chinn Ridge after Porter's repulse opened the door to disaster. Col. Nathaniel McLean firmly believed that he could have held Chinn Ridge with Reynolds's division, and he blamed McDowell. McDowell had simply miscalculated and overreacted to the repulse of Porter's attack against Jackson. McDowell's decision to remove Reynolds's division from Chinn Ridge was "the great mistake" of the battle in McLean's opinion.[5]

None of the shortcomings of the Confederate attack would have mattered had McLean's Ohio Brigade faltered on Chinn Ridge. General Pope praised the Buckeyes for their "supreme gallantry and tenacity." Tower's brigade is equally deserving of praise, coming onto the field under fire as it did when all was in confusion yet remaining firm and stoutly resisting Kemper's division. Pope gratefully recalled,

> The conduct of these two brigades and their commanders in plain view of our whole left was especially distinguished, and called forth hearty and enthusiastic cheers. Their example was of great service and seemed to infuse new spirit into the troops that witnessed their intrepid conduct.[6]

But perhaps the most meaningful praise for the Union defenders on Chinn Ridge came from an unlikely source. The 5th Texas's Pvt. William Fletcher simply wrote, "The bluecoats on the ridge were a tough set to move."[7]

Appendix A
ORDER OF BATTLE

U.S. ARMY OF VIRGINIA
Maj. Gen. John Pope

I CORPS / MAJ. GEN. FRANZ SIGEL
    First Division / Brig. Gen. Robert Schenck
        First Brigade / Brig. Gen. Julius S. Stahel
            8th New York
            41st New York
            45th New York
            27th Pennsylvania
            2nd Battery, (Schirmer's) New York Light Artillery
        Second Brigade / Col. Nathaniel C. McLean
            25th Ohio
            55th Ohio
            73rd Ohio
            75th Ohio
            Battery K, 1st (Haskins's) Ohio Light Artillery

    Second Division / Brig. Gen. A. von Steinwehr
        First Brigade / Col. John A. Koltes
            29th New York
            68th New York
            73rd New York

Company C, 3rd West Virginia Cavalry

Battery I, 1st (Dilger's) Ohio Light Artillery

Reserve Artillery / Capt. Louis Schirmer

Battery I, 1st (Wiedrich's) New York Light Artillery

13th Battery, (Dieckmann's) New York Light Artillery

Battery C, (Hill's) West Virginia Light Artillery

Third Division / Brig. Gen. Carl Schurz

First Brigade / Col. Alexander Schimmelfennig

61st Ohio

74th Pennsylvania

8th West Virginia

Battery F, (Hampton's) Pennsylvania Light Artillery

Second Brigade / Col. Wlademier Krzyzanowski

54th New York

58th New York

75th Pennsylvania

Battery L, 2nd (Roemer's) New York Light Artillery

Independent Brigade / Brig. Gen. Robert H. Milroy

82nd Ohio

2nd West Virginia

3rd West Virginia

5th West Virginia

12th Battery, (Johnson's) Ohio Light Artillery

Companies C, E, L, 1st West Virginia Cavalry

II CORPS / MAJ. GEN. NATHANIEL P. BANKS

First Division / Brig. Gen. Alpheus S. Williams

First Brigade / Brig. Gen. Samuel W. Crawford

5th Connecticut

10th Maine

28th New York

46th Pennsylvania

Third Brigade / Brig. Gen. George H. Gordon

27th Indiana

2nd Massachusetts

3rd Wisconsin

Second Division / Brig. Gen. George S. Greene
  First Brigade / Col. Charles Candy
    5th Ohio
    7th Ohio
    29th Ohio
    66th Ohio
    28th Pennsylvania
  Second Brigade / Col. D. P. DeWitt
    3rd Maryland
    102nd New York
    109th Pennsylvania
    111th Pennsylvania
    8th & 12th U.S. Infantry
  Third Brigade / Col. James Tait
    3rd Delaware
    1st District of Columbia
    60th New York
    78th New York
    Purnell Legion
II Corps Artillery
    4th Battery, (Robinson's) Maine Light Artillery
    6th Battery, (McGilvery's) Maine Light Artillery
    Battery M, 1st (Cothram's) New York Light Artillery
    10th Battery, (Bruen's) New York Light Artillery
    Battery E, (Knap's) Pennsylvania Light Artillery
    Battery F, 4th (Muhlenberg's) U.S. Artillery

III CORPS / MAJ. GEN. IRVIN MCDOWELL
  First Division / Brig. Gen. John Hatch
  First Brigade / Col. Timothy Sullivan
    22nd New York
    24th New York
    30th New York
    84th New York
    2nd U.S. Sharpshooters
  Second Brigade / Brig. Gen. Abner Doubleday
    56th Pennsylvania

76th New York

95th New York

Third Brigade / Brig. Gen. Marsena R. Patrick

21st New York

23rd New York

35th New York

80th New York

Fourth Brigade / Brig. Gen. John B. Gibbon

19th Indiana

2nd Wisconsin

6th Wisconsin

7th Wisconsin

First Division Artillery

1st Battery, (Gerrish's) New Hampshire Light Artillery

Battery L, 1st (Reynolds's) New York Light Artillery

Battery D, 1st (Monroe's) Rhode Island Light Artillery

Battery B, 4th (Campbell's) U.S. Artillery

Second Division / Brig. Gen. James B. Ricketts

First Brigade / Brig. Gen. Abram Duryea

97th New York

104th New York

105th New York

107th New York

Second Brigade / Brig. Gen. Zealous B. Tower

26th New York

94th New York

88th Pennsylvania

90th Pennsylvania

Third Brigade / Col. John W. Stiles

12th Massachusetts

13th Massachusetts

83rd New York

11th Pennsylvania

Fourth Brigade / Col. Joseph Thoburn

7th Indiana

84th Pennsylvania

110th Pennsylvania

1st West Virginia

Second Division Artillery

  2nd Battery, (Hall's) Maine Light Artillery

  5th Battery, (Leppien's) Maine Light Artillery

  Battery F, 1st (Matthews's) Pennsylvania Light Artillery

  Battery C, (Thompson's) Pennsylvania Light Artillery

Reynolds's Division / Brig. Gen. John F. Reynolds

  First Brigade / Brig. Gen. George G. Meade

    3rd Pennsylvania Reserves

    4th Pennsylvania Reserves

    7th Pennsylvania Reserves

    8th Pennsylvania Reserves

    13th Pennsylvania Reserves

  Second Brigade / Brig. Gen. Truman Seymour

    1st Pennsylvania Reserves

    2nd Pennsylvania Reserves

    5th Pennsylvania Reserves

    6th Pennsylvania Reserves

  Third Brigade / Brig. Gen. Conrad F. Jackson, Col. Martin Hardin

    9th Pennsylvania Reserves

    10th Pennsylvania Reserves

    11th Pennsylvania Reserves

    12th Pennsylvania Reserves

  Reynolds's Division Artillery

    Battery A, 1st (Simpson's) Pennsylvania Light Artillery

    Battery B, 1st (Cooper's) Pennsylvania Light Artillery

    Battery G, 1st (Kerns's) Pennsylvania Light Artillery

    Battery C, 5th (Ransom's) U.S. Artillery

II Corps Artillery

  16th Battery, (Naylor's) Indiana Light Artillery

  6th Battery, (McGilvery's) Maine Light Artillery

Piatt's Brigade / Brig. Gen. A. Sanders Piatt

  63rd Indiana

  86th New York

Cavalry / Col. John Beardsley
  1st Connecticut Cavalry Battalion
  1st Maryland Cavalry
  4th New York Cavalry
  9th New York Cavalry
  6th Ohio Cavalry
II Corps Cavalry / Brig. Gen. John Buford
  1st Michigan Cavalry
  5th New York Cavalry
  1st Vermont Cavalry
  1st West Virginia Cavalry
III Corps Cavalry / Brig. Gen. George D. Bayard
  1st Maine Cavalry
  1st New Jersey Cavalry
  2nd New York Cavalry
  1st Pennsylvania Cavalry
  1st Rhode Island Cavalry

U. S. ARMY OF THE POTOMAC

III CORPS / MAJ. GEN. SAMUEL P. HEINTZELMAN
  First Division / Maj. Gen. Phil Kearney
    First Brigade / Brig. Gen. John C. Robinson
      20th Indiana
      63rd Pennsylvania
      105th Pennsylvania
    Second Brigade / Brig. Gen. David B. Birney
      3rd Maine
      4th Maine
      1st New York
      38th New York
      40th New York
      101st New York
      57th Pennsylvania
    Third Brigade / Col. Orlando M. Poe
      2nd Michigan
      3rd Michigan

5th Michigan
37th New York
99th Pennsylvania
First Division Artillery
  Battery E, 1st (Randolph's) Rhone Island Light Artillery
  Battery K, 1st (Graham's) U.S. Artillery

Second Division / Maj. Gen. Joseph Hooker
  First Brigade / Brig. Gen. Cuvier Grover
    1st Massachusetts
    11th Massachusetts
    16th Massachusetts
    2nd New Hampshire
    26th Pennsylvania
  Second Brigade / Col. Nelson Taylor
    70th New York
    71st New York
    72nd New York
    73rd New York
    74th New York
  Third Brigade / Col. Joseph Carr
    5th New Jersey
    6th New Jersey
    7th New Jersey
    8th New Jersey
    2nd New York
    115th Pennsylvania

V CORPS / MAJ. GEN. FITZ JOHN PORTER
  First Division / Maj. Gen. George W. Morell
    First Brigade / Col. Charles W. Roberts
      2nd Maine
      18th Massachusetts
      22nd Massachusetts
      1st Michigan
      13th New York
      25th New York

Second Brigade / Brig. Gen. Charles Griffin
  9th Massachusetts
  32nd Massachusetts
  4th Michigan
  14th New York
  62nd Pennsylvania
Third Brigade / Brig. Gen. Daniel Butterfield
  16th Michigan
  Michigan Sharpshooters
  12th New York
  17th New York
  44th New York
  83rd Pennsylvania
  1st U.S. Sharpshooters
First Division Artillery
  3rd Battery, (Martin's) Massachusetts Light Artillery
  Battery C, 1st (Waterman's) Rhode Island Light Artillery
  Battery D, 5th (Hazlett's) U.S. Artillery

Second Division / Brig. Gen. George Sykes
  First Brigade / Lt. Col. Robert C. Buchanan
    3rd U.S.
    4th U.S.
    12th U.S.
    14th U.S.
  Second Brigade / Lt. Col. William Chapman
    1st U.S.
    2nd/10th U.S.
    6th U.S.
    11th U.S.
    17th U.S.
  Third Brigade / Col. Gouverneur K. Warren
    5th New York
    10th New York
  Second Division Artillery
    Batteries E&G, 1st (Randol's) U.S. Artillery
    Battery K, 5th (Smead's) U.S. Artillery
    Battery I, 5th (Weed's) U.S. Artillery

IX CORPS / MAJ. GEN. JESSE RENO
First Division / Brig. Gen. Isaac Stevens
First Brigade / Col. Benjamin C. Christ
8th Michigan
50th Pennsylvania
Second Brigade / Col. Daniel Leasure
46th New York
100th Pennsylvania
Third Brigade / Col. Addison Farnsworth
28th Massachusetts
79th New York
First Division Artillery
8th Battery, (Cook's) Massachusetts Light Artillery
Battery E, 2nd (Benjamin's) U.S. Artillery

Second Division / Maj. Gen. Jesse Reno
First Brigade / Col. James Nagle
2nd Maryland
6th New Hampshire
48th Pennsylvania
Second Brigade / Col. Edward Ferrero
21st Massachusetts
51st New York
51st Pennsylvania
Kanawha Division Detachment
30th Ohio
36th Ohio

ARMY OF NORTHERN VIRGINIA
General Robert E. Lee

LONGSTREET'S COMMAND / MAJ. GEN. JAMES LONGSTREET
Jones' Division / Brig. Gen. David R. Jones
Toombs' Brigade / Col. Henry L. Benning
2nd Georgia
15th Georgia
17th Georgia
20th Georgia

Drayton's Brigade / Brig. Gen. Thomas F. Drayton
   50th Georgia
   51st Georgia
   15th South Carolina
   Phillips Legion
Jones's Brigade / Col. George T. Anderson
   1st Georgia
   7th Georgia
   8th Georgia
   9th Georgia
   11th Georgia

Wilcox's Division / Brig. Gen. Cadmus M. Wilcox
   Wilcox's Brigade / Brig. Gen. Cadmus M. Wilcox
      8th Alabama
      9th Alabama
      10th Alabama
      11th Alabama
      Richmond (Anderson's) Virginia Artillery
   Featherston's Brigade / Brig. Gen. Winfield S. Featherston
      12th Mississippi
      16th Mississippi
      19th Mississippi
      2nd Mississippi Battalion
      Dixie (Chapman's) Virginia Artillery
   Pryor's Brigade / Brig. Gen. Roger A. Pryor
      14th Alabama
      2nd Florida
      5th Florida
      8th Florida
      3rd Virginia

Kemper's Division / Brig. Gen. James L. Kemper
   Kemper's Brigade / Col. Montgomery D. Corse
      1st Virginia
      7th Virginia
      11th Virginia
      17th Virginia
      24th Virginia

Jenkins's Brigade / Brig. Gen. Micah Jenkins
  1st South Carolina Volunteers
  2nd South Carolina (Rifles)
  5th South Carolina
  6th South Carolina
  4th South Carolina Battalion
  Palmetto Sharpshooters
Pickett's Brigade / Col. Eppa Hunton
  8th Virginia
  18th Virginia
  19th Virginia
  28th Virginia
  56th Virginia

Hood's Division / Brig. Gen. John B. Hood
  Texas Brigade / Brig. Gen. John B. Hood
    1st Texas
    4th Texas
    5th Texas
    18th Georgia
    Hampton Legion
  Law's Brigade / Col. Evander M. Law
    4th Alabama
    2nd Mississippi
    11th Mississippi
    6th North Carolina
  Hood's Division Artillery / Bushrod W. Froebel
    Charleston German (Bachman's) South Carolina Artillery
    Palmetto (Garden's) South Carolina Artillery
    Rowan (Reilly's) North Carolina Artillery
  Evans's Independent Brigade / Brig. Gen. Nathan G. Evans
    17th South Carolina
    18th South Carolina
    22nd South Carolina
    23rd South Carolina
  Holcombe Legion
  Macbeth (Boyce's) South Carolina Artillery
  Longstreet's Artillery Reserve

Washington Artillery / Col. John B. Walton
Squires's 1st Company
Richardson's 2nd Company
Miller's 3rd Company
Eshleman's 4th Company
Other Artillery
Goochland (Turner's) Virginia Battery
Donaldsonville (Maurin's) Louisiana Artillery
Loudoun (Rogers's) Virginia Artillery
Fauquier (Stribling's) Virginia Artillery

Anderson's Division / Maj. Gen. Richard H. Anderson
Armistead's Brigade / Brig. Gen. Lewis A. Armistead
9th Virginia
14th Virginia
38th Virginia
53rd Virginia
57th Virginia
5th Virginia Battalion
Mahone's Brigade / Brig. Gen. William Mahone
6th Virginia
12th Virginia
16th Virginia
41st Virginia
Wright's Brigade / Brig. Gen. Ambrose R. Wright
44th Alabama
3rd Georgia
22nd Georgia
48th Georgia
Anderson's Division Artillery
Lee's Battalion / Col. Stephen D. Lee
Bath (Taylor's) Virginia Artillery
Portsmouth (Grimes's) Virginia Artillery
Bedford (Jordan's) Virginia Artillery
Richmond (Parker's) Virginia Artillery
Rhett's South Carolina Battery
Ashland (Woolfolk's) Virginia Artillery

Other Artillery
   Norfolk (Huger's) Virginia Artillery
   Lynchburg Beauregard (Moorman's) Virginia Artillery

JACKSON'S COMMAND / MAJ. GEN. THOMAS J. "STONEWALL" JACKSON
   Jackson's Division / Brig. Gen. William E. Starke
      Stonewall Brigade / Col. William S. H. Baylor
         2nd Virginia
         4th Virginia
         5th Virginia
         27th Virginia
         33rd Virginia
      Second Brigade / Col. Bradley T. Johnson
         21st Virginia
         42nd Virginia
         48th Virginia
         1st Virginia Battalion
      Taliaferro's Brigade / Col. Alexander G. Taliaferro
         10th Virginia
         23rd Virginia
         37th Virginia
         47th Alabama
         48th Alabama
      Louisiana Brigade / Col. Leroy A. Stafford
         1st Louisiana
         2nd Louisiana
         9th Louisiana
         10th Louisiana
         15th Louisiana
      Coppens's Louisiana Battalion
      Jackson's Division Artillery / Maj. L. M. Shumaker
      Allegheny (Carpenter's) Virginia Artillery
      Baltimore (Brockenbrough's) 2nd Maryland Battery
      Richmond Hampden (Caskie's) Virginia Artillery
      Winchester (Cutshaw's) Virginia Artillery
      Rockbridge (Poague's) Virginia Artillery
      Lynchburg Lee (Raines's) Virginia Artillery

Page-Shenandoah Eighth Star Virginia Artillery
Danville (Schumaker's) Virginia Artillery

Ewell's Division / Brig. Gen. Alexander R. Lawton
  Lawton's Brigade / Col. Marcellus Douglass
    13th Georgia
    26th Georgia
    31st Georgia
    38th Georgia
    60th Georgia
    61st Georgia
  Trimble's Brigade / Capt. W. F. Brown
    15th Alabama
    12th Georgia
    21st Georgia
    21st North Carolina
    1st North Carolina Battalion
  Hays's (Forno's) Brigade / Col. H. B. Strong
    5th Louisiana
    6th Louisiana
    7th Louisiana
    8th Louisiana
    14th Louisiana
  Early's Brigade / Brig. Gen. Jubal Early
    13th Virginia
    25th Virginia
    31st Virginia
    44th Virginia
    52nd Virginia
    58th Virginia
  Ewell's Division Artillery / Maj. A. R. Courtney
  Staunton (Balthis's) Virginia Artillery
  Chesapeake (Brown's) 4th Maryland Battery
  Louisiana Guard (D'Aquin's) Artillery
  Andrews's 1st Maryland Battery
  Bedford (Johnson's) Virginia Artillery
  Richmond Henrico (Courtney's) Virginia Artillery

A. P. Hill's "Light" Division / Maj. Gen. Ambrose P. Hill
  Branch's Brigade / Brig. Gen. Lawrence O. Branch
    7th North Carolina
    18th North Carolina
    28th North Carolina
    33rd North Carolina
    37th North Carolina
  Pender's Brigade / Brig. Gen. W. Dorsey Pender
    16th North Carolina
    22nd North Carolina
    34th North Carolina
    38th North Carolina
  Gregg's Brigade / Brig. Gen. Maxcy Gregg
    1st South Carolina
    12th South Carolina
    13th South Carolina
    14th South Carolina
    Orr's Rifles
  Archer's Brigade / Brig. Gen. James J. Archer
    19th Georgia
    1st Tennessee
    7th Tennessee
    14th Tennessee
    5th Alabama Battalion
  Field's Brigade / Col. J. M. Brockenbrough
    40th Virginia
    47th Virginia
    55th Virginia
    22nd Virginia Battalion
  Thomas's Brigade / Col. Edward L. Thomas
    14th Georgia
    35th Georgia
    45th Georgia
    49th Georgia
  A. P. Hill's "Light" Division Artillery / Lt. Col. R. L. Walker
    Fredericksburg (Braxton's) Virginia Artillery
    Richmond (Crenshaw's) Virginia Battery

Richmond Letcher (Davidson's) Virginia Artillery
Branch (Latham's) North Carolina Artillery
Middlesex (Fleet's) Virginia Artillery
Pee Dee (McIntosh's) South Carolina Artillery
Richmond Purcell (Parker's) Virginia Artillery

Cavalry Division / Maj. Gen. James E. B. Stuart
    Lee's Brigade / Brig. Gen. Fitz Lee
        1st Virginia Cavalry
        3rd Virginia Cavalry
        4th Virginia Cavalry
        5th Virginia Cavalry
        9th Virginia Cavalry
    Brig. Gen. Beverly Robertson
        2nd Virginia Cavalry
        6th Virginia Cavalry
        7th Virginia Cavalry
        12th Virginia Cavalry
        17th Virginia Cavalry Battalion
    Stuart Horse Artillery
        1st Company Stuart (Pelham's) Horse Artillery

Appendix B
Tour Guide for Longstreet's Attack

Visitors to Manassas National Battlefield must remember that the National Park Service primarily interprets the First Battle of Bull Run. The year-round visitor center located on Henry Hill is devoted almost exclusively to that campaign. The park's layout is not always user friendly for visitors seeking to follow the course of the Second Battle of Manassas in the same way as at other popular battlefields such as Antietam, Gettysburg, and Chickamauga. Nevertheless, this battle offers the Civil War enthusiasts much more "fodder" in terms of personalities, drama, and military history than what the battlefield visitor center might lead one to believe. Touring the Second Battle also offers the opportunity to view a battlefield in a more natural setting, one that lacks the intrusive monuments that dominate some others.

Before getting into the tour itself, here are some hints to maximizing your experience at Manassas National Battlefield. This island of historical drama and natural beauty is situated on nearly five thousand acres of land, in the midst of the ever-growing suburban sprawl of northern Virginia. Fortunately most of the sites related to Second Manassas are isolated from the traffic, and once on the battlefield, you will scarcely notice the several major transportation routes around you. However, this factor requires that visitors time their tour to avoid the morning and evening rush hours, for both safety and practical matters. Since traffic through the park is heavy at all times, the utmost caution must be maintained and all traffic and pedestrian rules obeyed.

It is recommended that you first stop at the visitor center to learn about any changes to or situations concerning roads and trails, or other issues that could impact your touring. Additionally, you should ask the park service rangers if the Stuart's Hill Center is open and if the Dogan House area can be accessed, as they are not open on a regular basis.

As you tour any section of the Manassas Battlefield, it is important to understand the differences between the modern and historical landscapes. As a general rule, ground cover has changed greatly in most areas of the park. What is today predominately a woodland was known as the Plains of Manassas during the Civil War. At that time, the area consisted of many farms, which contained pastures and cropland. Trees existed primarily as borders along the various waterways, although there were several large woods as well. As a result of the more open terrain during the 1860s, the soldiers had the advantage of being able to see what was happening at more distant points that are now blocked from our view by forests.

Finally, a word on the structure of this tour is in order. Although a vehicle will be needed, learning about Second Manassas should, if possible, include a walking tour of the assault path, a distance of about 1.7 miles as the crow flies and not counting a return hike. Simply driving from one stop to another does not give you the opportunity to visit all scenes of crucial action. The stops are designed as waypoints, but this guide provides information for tourists to take in as they move from stop to stop.

Walking the path of Longstreet's assault is the best way to understand what happened on August 30, 1862, and how the terrain affected the battle. To avoid backtracking on foot, it is recommended that two vehicles be utilized if possible. One should be parked at the Henry Hill visitor center parking lot to be retrieved at the end of the walking tour, and the other can be used to drive to the starting point of the walking tour. (If you don't mind the extra hiking, you can simply walk from the visitor center to the starting point on foot.) There is also the option of taking an alternative loop back to your starting point that covers different trails and areas of Longstreet's attack not previously traversed. In fact, many will enjoy taking the optional return loop even if it is not necessary to view some more "seldom seen" sights at Manassas National Battlefield.

STOP 1: LEWIS HOUSE

From the driveway to the visitor center, turn right (north) on Sudley Road, Route 234. Proceed to the traffic light at the Stone House intersection. Turn left here onto U.S. Route 29 (west), known as the Warrenton Turnpike during the Civil War. Pass New York Avenue on your left and the Confederate Cemetery on your right. At Groveton Road, turn left. Proceed south on Groveton Road, which was known as Lewis Lane during the war. Make a right on Pageland Lane. This turn is the last right turn you can take before reaching the overpass for I-66. Pageland Lane bends sharply to the left and then back to the right. After the right bend, pull off in the entranceway at the gate to the park service road. The copse of trees atop the slight knoll immediately south of this entrance marks the Lewis House. Walk to the trees and view the interpretive sign.

You are in the center of Longstreet's battle line as it stood immediately prior to the attack. His battle line was facing eastward, which is to your left when you face I-66. Kemper's division occupied the grounds on both sides of the Lewis House. D. R. Jones's division formed up on Kemper's right and would have been in position on the opposite side of the interstate. As you face eastward from Kemper's position, Hood's division would be off to your left in the lower ground near U.S. 29, the wartime Warrenton Turnpike.

STOP 2: NEW YORK AVENUE

Return to your vehicle. Turn around and go back to Groveton Road where you will turn left. Proceed to U.S. 29 and turn right (east) on that road. This intersection is the center of what was the crossroads hamlet of Groveton during the war. The building in the northwest quadrant of the intersection is all that remains in the park today.

As you head east on U.S. 29, you will pass the Confederate Cemetery on your left (north). Continue down the hill and then take the first available

LONGSTREET'S ATTACK TOUR

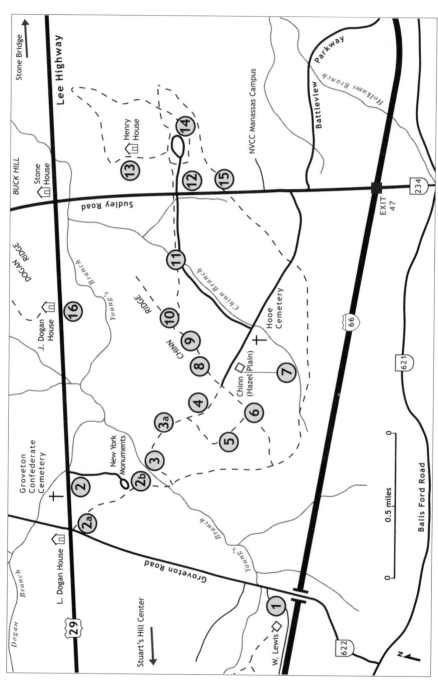

Chad Blevins

right turn onto New York Avenue. Pull into the parking lot on your immediate right. Ascend the hill to the monument and artillery, which is facing westward. The monument to the 14th Brooklyn Regiment is related to fighting on the evening of August 29. Upon this hill on August 30, Hazlett's battery resisted the advance of the 1st and 4th Texas on the left flank of Hood's brigade. They held this position until Warren's brigade was driven away farther to the left.

Proceed down the western slope of the hill to the opening in the fence along Groveton Road (stop 2A). Skirmishers from the 10th New York of Warren's brigade lined the fence along the road during the battle. Hood's Texans attacked from directly in front of you and quickly routed the New Yorkers out of their position and drove them back (eastward) in confusion into the woods in front of Warren's main line. Turn around and follow the trail that angles off to the southeast into the woods. This trail will eventually put you into position in front of the right flank of Hood's brigade, where the 5th Texas opened fire and decimated the 5th New York.

When you emerge from the woods, you will see a parking lot and the monuments to the 5th and 10th New York Zouaves of Warren's brigade (stop 2B). The monument in your immediate front honors the 10th New York, while the one farther to the left commemorates the sacrifices of the 5th New York at the Second Battle of Manassas. The ground on the ridge and the reverse slope was covered with the dead and wounded of Warren's brigade. After his men were driven off, Longstreet deployed several batteries on this ridge to support his attack against the Federals on Chinn Ridge. Remember that at the time of the battle, much of the wood lot east of the creek in the valley below was scrub pine. The artillerists were able to view events on Chinn Ridge from this location and provided artillery support to later stages of Longstreet's attack.

The trail to continue the path of Longstreet's assault is just beyond the 10th New York monument, which is located at the southern end of the parking lot. Walk along the walkway in front of the monuments until you reach the trail where you will turn left. As you proceed along the trail, it shortly angles off to the right as it slopes downward toward Young's Branch. From this area of the slope, the 5th Texas peppered Warren's men as they crossed the stream, causing it to run red from the blood of the Federals shot down in the water as they fled for their lives. Continue on down the trail until you reach the wooden bridge over Young's Branch. As you cross the bridge, notice that a path continues to the right of the bridge and up the opposite bank of the stream. This is a trace of the wartime remnant of Compton's Lane.

At this point in the battle, Hood's brigade encountered increasing Federal resistance from Hardin's brigade, which McDowell had rushed back to confront the Confederate attack. Hood attempted to rein in the Texas Brigade to coordinate its attack with the rest of Longstreet's wing. However, Lt. Col. John Upton of the 5th Texas was killed while crossing Young's Branch a short distance downstream from the bridge before he could order his wing of the regiment to halt.

Follow the trail a short distance straight ahead up a steep but short incline and then over a small wooden bridge until it turns sharply to the left. Continue for several hundred yards roughly paralleling the stream. After crossing a second wooden bridge over a normally dry gulley, proceed for approximately fifty yards until you reach an NPS trail marker. The trail will make a sharp ninety-degree turn to the right. Pause here.

STOP 3: YOUNG'S BRANCH

In this position, turn and look back toward Young's Branch. Warren's Zouaves streamed down the hillside on the opposite bank and then across the stream under heavy fire from Hood's brigade. In this area, the 18th Georgia captured the battle flag of the 10th New York. Now stand with your back to Young's Branch (which is west of your location) and look to your left front. You will initially notice a hollow and then rising ground in the woods beyond on the left side of the trail, which runs eastward from this point.

Upon that rising ground, which you will momentarily ascend on the trail, Col. Martin Hardin's brigade of Pennsylvania Reserves and Kerns's and Simpson's Pennsylvania batteries went into position. A few surviving New Yorkers rallied on Hardin's battle line. The Pennsylvanians initially stalled Hood's advance; however, the right wing of the 5th Texas advanced beyond the left (southern) flank of Hardin's battle line and eventually flanked the

Reserves out of this position as they advanced on your immediate right. A few hundred yards farther to your left, the 18th Georgia and 4th Texas overran and captured one of the Pennsylvania batteries commanded by the mortally wounded Captain Kerns. After this combat with the Pennsylvanians, the 1st and 4th Texas on Hood's left were ultimately brought back to this general area along Young's Branch after maneuvering through the pine thicket that covered the area during the war. Here they sat out the remainder of the battle.

Continue up (east) the trail toward Chinn Ridge until you come to the first crest (stop 3A). Hardin's left flank rested on the military crest of this ridge and was then attacked by the 5th Texas in this general area. Continue along the trail, where you will notice a very slight descent to a wet-weather stream. At the time of the war, the terrain to your left was generally covered with scrub pines and was relatively open to the view of the Federal infantry and artillery on Chinn's Ridge and Dogan Ridge. The area to the right was a hardwood forest and offered better concealment for the attacking Confederates. Proceed along the trail until you come to another wooden bridge. This small depression extends for hundreds of yards toward the Warrenton Turnpike, growing wider and deeper as it nears Young's Branch. Hood's brigade halted and lay down in the ravine much farther to the left, where it was deeper and provided shelter from Union artillery and small arms fire.

It was at this point that the 5th Texas, Hampton Legion, and 18th Georgia moved under cover of the ravine and pines into a wooded area that was dominated by hardwood trees rather than the scrub pines as they moved from left to right. These larger trees provided the Confederates with greater cover against the heavy Union fire directed at them. Upon entering the woods, the Texans initially reorganized and rested, but Wofford's Georgians and Gary's South Carolinians pushed forward until their left flank was covered by the trees. Proceed up the trail until you arrive in the open field on the western slope of Chinn Ridge.

STOP 4: FIRST ATTACKS AGAINST CHINN RIDGE

Continue far enough into the open ground so you can see around the trees on your left. Looking through the opening in the trees, you can see Chinn

Ridge, where McLean's Ohio Brigade and Wiedrich's New York battery were in position. Immediately in front of you was the position of the 73rd Ohio on McLean's left flank. The initial Confederate attack by Hood's brigade came out of the woods to your left against the center of McLean's line. The Hampton Legion and 18th Georgia focused their efforts on Wiedrich's battery in the center of the Federal brigade, but the Ohioans stood firm. Immediately following the repulse of Hood's advance, Evans's brigade, commanded by Col. Peter F. Stevens, arrived to carry on the fight. Elements of the 5th Texas joined the attack on Stevens's right flank in the very area you are now standing. Once again, the Ohioans on the ridge threw back the Confederate assault, and the South Carolinians and Texans returned to the shelter of the woods. Hood and Stevens rallied the men and sent them toward the ridge again. Virtually every field officer in Evans's brigade went down killed or wounded, and the South Carolinians were forced to retreat to the wood line where they opened fire against the Ohioans on the ridge.

Turn around and walk back into the woods. Follow the trail for approximately sixty-five yards until you come to a small trail leading into the woods to your left. The easiest way to locate this path is to count the number of erosion control beams that the park service has installed perpendicular across the main trail. The side trail is located exactly at the third erosion control beam. Turn left and follow that path until you come to its end. As you continue, this trail grows fainter for a short distance but is usually marked by a low growth of grass. These woods are generally very open with little undergrowth, so hiking through them is relatively easy. An intervening ridge should be on your left between you and Chinn Ridge. If you lose the trail, keep that intervening ridge on your immediate left, and you will soon run into the main trail. When you reach the main trail, which is also a utility road, turn left and follow it until you emerge at the edge of the woods.

STOP 5: KEMPER'S ATTACK

From this area, the Confederates eventually launched an attack that broke McLean's left flank. As you face the ridge from the edge of the woods, the left flank of Kemper's division would have emerged from the trees in this area. On the ridge to your left front, Cooper's Pennsylvania battery had been shelling the attacking Confederates, but lacking infantry support it limbered up and retreated upon the appearance of Kemper's division. Kemper's front line, constituted by Kemper's Virginians and Jenkins's South Carolinians, was unable to change its front quickly enough to attack McLean, who was situation farther to the left on the ridge; it continued over the ridge pursuing the withdrawing artillery into the valley of Chinn Branch beyond.

To your immediate left, however, Colonel Robertson's regrouped 5th Texas Infantry charged out of the woods and attacked McLean's left flank. Almost simultaneously, the Ohioans saw Corse's brigade deployed in Kemper's rear line advancing and changing front from a couple of hundred yards to your right. The Texans captured the caisson of Cooper's battery and drove the 73rd Ohio back upon the 26th New York of Tower's brigade, which had just arrived behind the Ohioans and was attempting to extend the Federal line to the south through the Chinn yard. Farther to the left where you first emerged from the woods before reversing course, Evans's South Carolinians rallied and joined the Texans in their successful attack, driving off the 25th Ohio and McLean's artillery support. Then Montgomery Corse's Virginia brigade in the second line of Kemper's division emerged from the woods to your immediate right, and upon reaching the crest of the ridge in your front, they changed front and bore down toward the left to support the 5th Texas.

STOP 6: CHINN RIDGE

Continue walking up the ridge until you reach the gravel road at the top. Near the end of this trail to your right, you will find the remains of an old livestock pen that attests to the area's agricultural heritage. Turn left on the gravel road, and walk toward the scattered pines and parking lot. This is a wartime road and was the lane that led from the Chinn House to Compton's Lane. Looking down the eastern slope of Chinn Ridge as you continue down the road, you will notice the open fields leading to Chinn Branch at the bottom of the gentle slope. Hunton's and Jenkins's brigades continued their advance straight ahead until they reached the branch. However, Corse wheeled his brigade to the left and set a course to the renewed Union resistance beyond the Chinn House. His Virginians swept through these fields in line of battle as they headed to attack the regrouping Federals.

Continue on the road along the ridge through the pines. To your right in the well-kept yard is the foundation of the Chinn House, which you will visit later. For now, continue a short distance down the road until you come to a gate that leads to a paved parking area. Maneuver through the gate and move beyond the pines. Then turn to your left, walk to the fence line, and look toward the woods. You are now viewing the battlefield from the perspective of the 73rd Ohio on McLean's left—looking at the position of the Confederates as they attacked McLean's brigade. This section of fence approximates the line of the 73rd Ohio, although it would have been positioned on the military crest slightly forward of where you are standing. Behind you on the reverse slope of the ridge, Zealous Tower formed his brigade in line of battle parallel to McLean's as it arrived on the field.

STOP 7: CHINN HOUSE

Turn around and walk into the enclosed Chinn yard. Proceed to the foundation—all that remains of the Chinn House. It stood in the center of the combat that ensued after McLean's left flank broke. If you stand facing the foundation (south) with your back toward the park road, you would have seen the 26th New York come up behind the left flank and rear of the 73rd Ohio (to your right) and pass directly through the yard in its attempt to support McLean's endangered flank. When the New Yorkers advanced in this area, only the far left wing of the regiment was able to open fire on the approaching Confederates, the right being masked by the Ohioans. The New Yorkers were subsequently swept away by the attacking Texans and South Carolinians as they drove the 73rd Ohio from the ridge.

As you look to the south beyond the yard, you are looking at the ground where first Corse's brigade and later Benning's brigade advanced toward the house. In the open ground to the right of the foundation (as you face it with your back to the road), a battery of the Washington Artillery of New Orleans went into position and supported the later stages of the Confederate attack.

In addition to the house, the Chinn yard contained several outbuildings at the time of the battle. These structures complicated maneuvering through the yard for both Union and Confederate troops. An apple orchard also existed in the vicinity of the pine trees at the west end of the yard. As you face the Chinn House with your back to the parking area, turn to your left (east). Hundreds of Texans and South Carolinians halted in the yard and fired at the retreating Ohioans and New Yorkers who raced down the eastern slope toward Chinn Branch. These Confederates paid little attention to what was going on farther up Chinn Ridge toward the Warrenton Turnpike.

Turn to your left again so you are facing north and the wooden fence in the distance. Notice the crest of Chinn Ridge just beyond the fence line. Behind this swelling high ground and out of sight of the Confederates in the Chinn yard, Col. John C. Lee ordered his 55th Ohio to change front toward the Chinn House. The Ohioans then charged and suddenly appeared on the crest of the ridge and opened a devastating enfilading fire into the left flank of Evans's South Carolinians and the 5th Texas as they advanced through the Chinn yard. The Confederates fled southward through the orchard and back into the woods to the west. The 55th Ohio then took up a static position behind the fence and battled Corse's brigade, which almost immediately came on the scene as it approached from the south and struggled to maneuver through the yard around the Chinn House and outbuildings. At this point, the axis of the action on Chinn Ridge changed from a west-to-east Confederate attack to a south-to-north assault path.

Tower's brigade soon came up on the new left flank of the Ohioans and extended the battle line along the fence line into the valley of Chinn Branch. Tower's Pennsylvanians and New Yorkers opened fire on Hunton's and Jenkins's brigades of Kemper's division, as those units belatedly turned around and attacked back up the southeastern slope of Chinn Ridge toward the new Federal line. This line roughly approximated the wooden fence line in the distance on the opposite side of the park road. On the ground immediately east of Chinn Branch, in the valley to your right, McDowell deployed the 83rd New York, which temporarily checked the advance of Jenkins's right wing on that side of the stream.

Return to the parking lot, turn to your left, and walk to the top of the ridge so that you are heading back toward McLean's original position. When you reach the position of the 73rd Ohio, turn to the right and follow the paved trail that runs along the crest of the ridge. As you do so, you are following the course of McLean's original battle line. There are park signs with quotes from soldiers as you continue along this trail.

STOP 8: THE FENCE LINE

Follow the trail along the crest of the ridge until you reach the fence line. As you proceed, you are walking in the footsteps of the Virginians, Georgians, and Mississippians as they attacked the various Union troops, who joined and replaced the 55th Ohio and Tower's brigade along the fence line. You are also approaching the position of the 55th Ohio after it changed front to repulse the Confederates who had swept most of McLean's brigade from the ridge. As the battle raged, the 12th and 13th Massachusetts came forward to support the Ohioans on their right flank, extending the line into what are now woods to your left.

Leppien's battery in the distance created substantial confusion in the Union battle line as it maneuvered into position. It was initially overrun by Corse's brigade but was recaptured by the Germans of the 41st New York. Eventually, the 11th Mississippi of Law's brigade reinforced Corse's left flank in this area and aided the Virginians in driving the Federals back and permanently securing Leppien's battery.

STOP 9: LEPPIEN'S BATTERY

Proceed along the trail until you reach the point where two guns are now posted to represent Leppien's battery. This was the position of his Maine battery. These guns accompanied Tower to Chinn Ridge and deployed when his brigade went into action. Face back toward the Chinn House. At the apex of the fighting on Chinn Ridge, the 55th Ohio was in line of battle along the fence line, battling Corse's Virginians, with the 88th and 90th Pennsylvania and 94th New York extending the line to the right. The 12th and 13th Massachusetts came up on their right and Tower's Pennsylvanians and New Yorkers to the left. Eventually, the 11th Pennsylvania reinforced the sagging Union battle line. The entire line gradually fell back toward the battery while enduring enormous casualties in the combat with the ever-growing Confederate attack force.

Confederate pressure grew, and the Union battle line grudgingly gave way, retreating from the fence line toward Leppien's guns. From the valley of Chinn Branch to your left, Jenkins's South Carolinians and Hunton's Virginians attacked the left flank, driving back the New Yorkers holding the low ground. The 11th Mississippi of Law's brigade charged out of the woods to your right front near the Chinn House. Directly in front of you, Corse reorganized his Virginians and attacked straight toward Leppien's guns. With pressure on both flanks of the Union line, the Confederates surged toward the guns. Corse's Virginians were the first in the battery, where Lt. Col. Frederick Skinner cut down several Federal gunners with his sword before being wounded in the melee for the guns, which fell to the Virginians.

Standing at the guns, face toward the rear of the position. From this direction, Union reinforcements quickly arrived on the scene shortly after the guns were overrun. The 41st New York and Koltes's brigade eventually recaptured the guns, driving off the victorious but disorganized Confederates beyond the Chinn House. The New Yorkers actually hauled several of the guns off the ridge toward the Stone House intersection. Krzyzanowski's brigade arrived on the scene, faced toward the woods, and battled Confederates from Law's brigade who attempted to get around Koltes's right flank.

Shortly after Koltes retook this position, the battery of the Washington artillery deployed near the Chinn House and opened fire on Koltes's line. Koltes, seeing the Confederate infantry in confusion, ordered a charge but was mortally wounded before it gained any momentum. At about the same time, Benning's brigade arrived from the south and joined the fray. The 20th Georgia deployed on the west side of the house, the 2nd Georgia on its east side. The 15th and 17th Georgia advanced through the valley of Chinn Branch. The appearance of Benning's organized battle line attracted the disordered Virginians, South Carolinians, Mississippians, and Texans who had been knocked back toward the Chinn House, giving structure to the large Confederate force on the ridge. The renewed advance soon swept the Federals from the ridge and recaptured all of Leppien's guns.

STOP 10: FLETCHER WEBSTER MONUMENT

Return to the trail and proceed from the battery position to the next marker. Follow the side trail to the right toward the stone monument. This monument was erected to Col. Fletcher Webster, son of Massachusetts senator Daniel Webster, who was mortally wounded on Chinn Ridge. He was wounded in the area to the right of Leppien's battery but was carried to this area after his fall. After viewing the monument, follow the trail down the east side of the ridge. The Confederates attacking with Benning's brigade advanced down the ridge, pursuing the retreating Federals toward Henry Hill and the Stone House intersection.

STOP 11: CHINN BRANCH

Follow the trail down the ridge to the park road. When you reach the road, turn to your left and walk along its side. The road soon crosses over Chinn Branch. During the battle, this stream attracted hundreds of wounded men seeking water and shelter. When the Confederates secured control of the ridge, the 2nd Georgia continued its advance along this stream toward the Stone House intersection. The rest of the troops with Benning turned to the east, descended Chinn Ridge, crossed the stream, and attacked Federal troops that Pope and McDowell had posted on Sudley Road to the east while the fighting raged on Chinn Ridge. Follow the park road back toward Sudley Road and the entrance to the park's visitor center on Henry Hill. You will ascend what is known as Bald Hill and into a ravine and then begin ascending Henry Hill. The combat that took place in this immediate sector between Milroy's brigade and Confederate units from D. R. Jones's and Kemper's divisions was furious. To your right, George T. Anderson's brigade attacked Chapman's Regulars, while back-and-forth combat between Benning's brigade and the Pennsylvania Reserves took place to your left. The Georgians first charged out of the woods on your left, crossed the road, and swept up Henry Hill, only to be driven back almost all the way to Chinn Branch. They in turn shoved the Pennsylvanians back into the cut of Sudley Road. When you reach Sudley Road, you may want to pass through the trees and into the open area on your left to view the ground over which the Confederates attacked Milroy's brigade.

Sudley Road served as a ready-made breastwork for the Union soldiers. From that position, the Federals repulsed several attacks by elements of Kemper's, Jones's, and Anderson's divisions. When you reach Sudley Road, stop and make sure that it is safe to cross. Cars pass rapidly through this area, and the utmost caution is essential.

STOP 12: SUDLEY ROAD CUT

After crossing the road and passing just beyond the park gate, turn to your right and walk through the field toward the woods for approximately fifty yards. You will now be walking parallel to the modern road and heading east toward Manassas. You will find a trail entrance into the woods about fifteen yards east from modern Sudley Road. Follow this trail for about twenty feet. You are standing in the wartime Sudley Road. It was only a winding wagon road that erosion had worn into a natural breastwork. Farther to the south toward I-66 and the commercial area, the old road trace can be followed on the west side of the road and is easily found by following the utility poles and lines, if so desired.

Your immediate position was occupied by the right of Chapman's brigade of the U.S. Regular Army. To your right, where the modern park entrance is located, was the left flank of Milroy's brigade of West Virginians and Ohioans. Turn and look toward Sudley Road, visualizing yourself as a Union soldier of Sykes's U.S. Regulars repulsing the Confederate efforts to seize Henry Hill. On the rise behind you, the 86th New York came up to provide support to the hard-pressed troops in the road cut. Several batteries of artillery also fired directly over the heads of the infantrymen in the road. At one point, the cannon were so close to the road that some U.S. Regulars complained about powder from the artillery burning the backs of their necks. This position eventually became untenable when Confederate artillery and Mahone's brigade flanked it farther to the left (southward) at the commercial area near the I-66 interchange. That portion of the battlefield where the Confederate artillery took position and where infantry attacked the left of the Union line is lost to commercial development. Buchanan's brigade of Regulars deployed in this area and fought a classic rear-guard action from this vicinity back to the crest of Henry Hill near the visitor center.

STOP 13: HENRY HOUSE

Proceed to the visitor center. From there, continue to the Henry House. The best place to observe the action of the Second Battle of Manassas in this area is in front of the house near the small cemetery. To better understand the Union troop deployments on the hill, turn and face the Henry House. To the right, Buchanan's brigade of U.S. Regulars was in position behind Milroy's brigade, which was in position down in the road cut. To the left, Ransom's battery was in position supported by two brigades of Brig. Gen. John Reynolds's Pennsylvania Reserves.

Turn and face the road. When the first wave of Confederate attacks hit, the 15th and 20th Georgia charged out of the woods, across Sudley Road directly in front of the house. At the same time, the 2nd Georgia closed in on the Sudley Road's vital intersection with the Warrenton Turnpike. Benning led the 15th and 20th Georgia up the hill toward Ransom's battery. As they neared the crest, Reynolds's Pennsylvanians came into view. The Federals charged and drove the Georgians down the hill and across the road into a skirt of woods that lined Chinn Branch. There the Georgians quickly rallied. The Pennsylvania Reserves followed the Confederates into the woods, where they encountered heavy gunfire. At the same time, the 2nd Georgia abandoned its drive on the intersection, changed direction, and struck Reynolds's right flank, driving the Pennsylvanians out of the woods in confusion. In the road cut just below the Henry House, Reynolds grabbed a battle flag and rallied the Reserves. The 3rd and 4th U.S. Infantry later went into position on the brow of the hill just above the road behind Milroy's brigade; Reynolds's troops and the Confederates abandoned any further efforts on Henry Hill or the intersection in this area. You may wish to walk down the road trace that leads toward Sudley Road and stand on the high ground above the road where the Regulars briefly went into position behind the Pennsylvanians.

STOP 14: HENRY HILL VISITOR CENTER

Return to the visitor center and proceed to the far side of the parking lot to the ground just beyond where the entrance road meets the parking area. The best place to interpret this action is in the general vicinity of Griffin's

Battery (related to First Manassas). This battery is located immediately east of the parking lot. By the time the Federals defending the road cut withdrew, Ferrero's IX Corps brigade had deployed in a semicircle facing the southern and eastern edges of the hill. The left of the brigade extended down the eastern slope of the hill into a ravine. Ferrero's men repulsed an attempt by Mahone's Virginians to attack the withdrawing Federal army and a half-hearted effort by the South Carolinians of Drayton's brigade, thereby effectively ending the Second Battle of Manassas. Pope retreated unmolested to Centreville that night and Lee held the battlefield, winning another victory for the Confederacy along the banks of Bull Run. His victory opened the door for the invasion of Maryland.

STOP 15 (OPTIONAL): RETURN LOOP

From Griffin's Battery, return to the pristine road-cut position located near the entranceway. Follow the road until it intersects the horse trail, which you will follow across Sudley Road. Again, as with all road intersections, use the utmost caution as traffic is extremely heavy and moving at a rapid pace well beyond posted speed limits. Follow the horse trail into the woods on the west side of the road. The trail will take you back over the ground that G. T. Anderson's brigade traversed on its way to attack the Sudley Road line. The high ground you ascend is Bald Hill.

You will eventually work your way back to a park road. Follow this road until you reach the Chinn Ridge area. When you reach the position of the 73rd Ohio, turn to your left and follow the road. Continue on the road until you reach the livestock pen. Do not return to the woods. This trail will soon intersect Compton's Lane, which you can follow back to the bridge that you first used to cross Young's Branch. Return to New York Avenue and your vehicle.

STOP 16 (OPTIONAL): DOGAN RIDGE

Dogan Ridge is usually closed on weekends. If you contact the park in advance or ask the ranger at the visitor center, you may be able to make arrangements to visit it if resources are available to open the gate. If so, the park ranger will then give you directions. There is an interpretive marker near the house that partially tells the story of the 45th New York. It is important to remember that the 45th New York first charged and drove off the 2nd Mississippi of Law's brigade before its retreat.

If you are unable to make arrangements, make a right turn on U.S. 29 when you depart New York Avenue. Proceed for three-tenths of a mile. At that point, turn on your right turn signal. At five tenths of a mile, pull off onto a large turn-off on the right side of the road. Turn on your flashers and remain in your car for safety reasons at this stop. Atop the hill to your left is the Dogan House, where Sigel's artillery was in position and fired at the Confederates as they attacked the Union troops stationed on Chinn Ridge to your right. In the later stages of the battle, the 2nd Mississippi charged up out of the bottom ground formed by Young's Branch to your right and rear. When they ascended the ridge in this area, the 45th New York counterattacked from its position near the Dogan House and drove the Mississippians down the ridge and into the woods beyond. The Germans of the 45th New York pursued, but were in turn repulsed and chased back up the ridge by the 4th Alabama and 6th North Carolina of Law's brigade. This attack was repulsed beyond the Dogan House by Dilger's battery and elements of the Iron Brigade. When you are done here, proceed with caution to reenter the road. Do not attempt to head westward but carefully reenter the highway and head eastward toward the Stone House intersection. You can turn around in the parking lot of the Stone House if you need to go west at this point.

Notes

Introduction
1. Hennessy, *Return to Bull Run*, 380.
2. Ibid., 456.
3. Ibid., 461.

Chapter 1. "Take Care of Yourself"
1. Luther B. Mesnard Memoirs, Firelands Historical Society, 14.
2. Sears, *To the Gates of Richmond*, 351.
3. Hennessy, *Return to Bull Run*, 15.
4. Dowdey, *Lee's Wartime Papers*, 239.
5. Hennessy, *Return to Bull Run*, 28.
6. Ibid., 30–31.
7. See Hennessy, *Return to Bull Run*, 35–49, for details on the maneuvers that led to Pope's withdrawal from the Rapidan line.
8. Hennessy, *Return to Bull Run*, 49–50.
9. Gold, *History of Clarke County, Virginia, and Its Connection with the War Between the States*, 178.
10. U.S. War Department, *The War of the Rebellion: A Compilation of the Official Records of the Union and Confederate Armies* (*OR* hereafter), 12:2:70–71.
11. Worsham, *One of Jackson's Foot Cavalry*, 78.
12. Marsena Patrick Diary, August 30, 1862, Library of Congress; Hood, *Advance and Retreat*, 35; *OR*, 12:3:741.
13. Samuel Heintzelman Journal, August 30, 1862, Library of Congress.
14. *OR*, 12:2:394; George Ruggles to Fitz John Porter, June 10, 1877, Fitz John Porter Papers, Library of Congress; *Proceedings and Report of the Board of Army Officers in the Case of Fitz John Porter*, 2, 311; Hennessy, *Second Manassas Battlefield Map Study*, 277–78, 302.
15. *OR*, 12:2:268, 286, 291.
16. Vautier, *History of the 88th Pennsylvania Volunteers*, 54–55.

17. E. H. Allen to T. C. H. Smith, illegible date, T. C. H. Smith Papers, Ohio Historical Society (OHS hereafter); *OR* 12:2:281, 286.

18. Warner, *Generals in Blue*, 304; Gatell, "John McLean," in Friedman and Israel, *Justices of the United States Supreme Court*, 544–45.

19. At Second Manassas, McLean's brigade comprised the 25th, 55th, 73rd, and 75th Ohio Infantry Regiments. For the most part, McLean's brigade lacked combat experience. Only the 25th Ohio had significant combat experience, having fought pitched engagements at Camp Allegheny in western Virginia on December 13, 1861, losing eighty-four men killed and wounded; at Mc-Dowell on May 8, 1862, losing fifty-seven men killed and wounded; and at Cross Keys on June 8, 1862, when the regiment lost sixty men killed and wounded. The 75th Ohio fought at McDowell, where it suffered the loss of thirty-eight men killed and wounded. At Second Manassas, the 55th and 73rd Ohio were untested regiments. Their combat experience consisted of skirmishing on the fringe of small battles such as McDowell and Cross Keys. McLean's units represented virtually every section of Ohio. The 25th Ohio was raised primarily in eastern Ohio, including companies from Steubenville, St. Clairsville, and Woodsfield. Counties in northern Ohio also contributed a large number of men from Toledo, Freemont, and Mansfield. The 55th Ohio was recruited from Ohio's North Coast between Cleveland and Toledo, as well as from the adjoining counties to the south. The 73rd Ohio was raised almost exclusively from the town of Chillicothe and the surrounding area. The Ohio River town of Marietta also sent men to this regiment. The 75th Ohio was recruited in southern Ohio, including companies from Athens, Columbus, Cincinnati, and Dayton. *OR*, 12:1:467.

20. Nathaniel C. McLean to John C. Ropes, October 6, 1897, John C. Ropes Papers, Boston University.

21. Reynolds reported that "the commanding general" ordered him off Chinn Ridge. The referral to a "commanding general" may have been a reference to Pope. If Pope ordered McDowell to remove Reynolds from Chinn Ridge, then the army commander deserves censure for another critical blunder during the battle. "From the Pennsylvania Reserves," *Lancaster Daily Express*, September 10, 1862.

22. *OR*, 12:2:286–95; Nathaniel C. McLean to John C. Ropes, October 6, 1897, John C. Ropes Papers, Boston University.

23. In stark contrast to McLean's behavior on August 30, 1862, Maj. Gen. George W. Morell marched part of his division to Centreville in error. Upon realizing his error, he remained where he was, making no effort to rejoin the army on the battlefield. Nathaniel C. McLean to John C. Ropes, October 6, 1897, John C. Ropes Papers, Boston University; Sherman, *Memoirs of General W. T. Sherman*, 887.

24. Conversation between Robert Schenck and T. C. H. Smith, August 30, 1864, T. C. H. Smith Papers, OHS.

Chapter 2. "Frenzied in Their Passions"

1. Charles Marshall's Testimony, *Proceedings and Report of the Board of Army Officers in the Case of Fitz John Porter*, 2, 212; James Longstreet, "Our March Against

Pope," in Buel and Johnston, *Battles and Leaders of the Civil War,* 2:521; Long-street, *From Manassas to Appomattox,* 184.

2. Johnston, *Four Years a Soldier,* 177; *OR,* 12:2:613.
3. Longstreet, "Our March Against Pope," in Buel and Johnston, *Battles and Leaders,* 2:521.
4. Longstreet, *From Manassas to Appomattox,* 188; http://www.johnbellhood .org/bio-01.htm, accessed March 23, 2011.
5. J. H. L., "Hood, Feeling the Enemy," contained in Buel and Johnston, *Battles and Leaders,* 2:276; General R. E. Lee to General Lewis T. Wigfall, *Houston Tri-Weekly Telegraph,* September 21, 1862.
6. Hood placed the Texas Brigade under Sellers's control when Longstreet summoned Hood to his headquarters at the outset of the attack. *OR,* 12:1:922; Hood, *Advance and Retreat,* 37.
7. Hennessy, *Second Manassas Battlefield Map Study,* map 12.
8. R. H. Leonard, "Texians at Manassas," *Houston Tri-Weekly Telegraph,* November 28, 1862.
9. Robert Campbell Diary, 83, Manassas National Battlefield Park (MNBP hereafter).
10. The withdrawal of Reynolds's division referred to by Warren is not when McDowell pulled the Pennsylvanians from Chinn Ridge. Warren is referring to when Reynolds fell back several hours earlier from his advanced position near Groveton to Chinn Ridge. This was the position occupied by Reynolds when he detected Longstreet's presence on the Union left. Hennessy, *Second Manassas Battlefield Map Study,* map 12; *OR,* 12:2:503–5.
11. Dawes, *Service with the Sixth Wisconsin Volunteers,* 69.
12. *OR* 12:2:490; C. G. H., "Camp Life in Virginia," *Cleveland Plain Dealer,* November 4, 1862.
13. Leonard, "Texians at Manassas"; *OR,* 12:2:505.
14. Ibid.
15. Alfred Davenport to his family, September 5, 1862, Alfred Davenport Papers, New York Historical Society.
16. Hennessy, *Return to Bull Run,* 370; Leonard, "Texians at Manassas."
17. *OR,* 12:2:609, 617–18; Campbell Diary, 84, MNBP; Leonard, "Texians at Manassas"; Nicholas Pomeroy Letters, Hill Jr. College History Complex.
18. Hennessy, *Return to Bull Run,* 371–72; *OR,* 12:2:613.
19. Dougherty, "An Eyewitness Account of Second Bull Run," 42.
20. Hood, *Advance and Retreat,* 36; M. V. Smith Reminiscences, Fredericksburg and Spotsylvania National Military Park (FSNMP hereafter), 17.
21. Robert H. Milroy to his wife, September 4, 1862, in Paulus, *Papers of General Robert Huston Milroy,* 1, 91–92.
22. J. Taggart Memoirs, Pennsylvania History and Museum Commission; Hardin, *History of the Twelfth Regiment,* 99–101.
23. According to Brig. Gen. John F. Reynolds, Simpson's and Cooper's batteries also deployed and resisted Hood's advance south of the Warrenton Turnpike. Lt. J. S. Fullerton of Cooper's battery wrote, "One half minute more and we would have lost our guns again. We fired our last round of ammunition, they captured our caissons again." They had previously lost their guns

during the Seven Days Battles for Richmond. As for Simpson's guns, it is known that a battery retreated through the 55th Ohio from the position Hardin and Kerns occupied. As the Texans captured all of Kerns's guns, I have concluded that Simpson's battery was on the hill with Hardin and Kerns, and was the battery that retreated through the 55th Ohio. Colonel Robertson also reported that the 5th Texas advanced "under a murderous fire from two of the enemy's batteries" during this phase of the battle. Hardin, *History of the Twelfth Regiment*, 100–1; *OR*, 12:2:394–95, 618; Mesnard Memoirs, 12, Firelands Historical Society.

24. *OR*, 12:2:615.
25. A member of the Texas Brigade wrote that Kerns was attempting to operate the guns alone. But a contemporary account by a Pennsylvanian in the *Cumberland Valley Spirit* revealed that Kerns was wounded and placed on a caisson, and that was struck by a Confederate shell. Polley, *Hood's Texas Brigade*, 90, 93; Polley, *A Soldier's Letters*, 75. Letter of Kennedy dated September 7, 1862, *Cumberland Valley Spirit*, September 24, 1996; *OR*, 12:2:615.
26. C.D.R. to editor, October 9, 1862, *Wyandot Pioneer*, October 17, 1862.
27. *OR*, 12:2:291.
28. Abraham Rudisill Papers, United States Army Military History Institute (USAMHI hereafter).
29. The description of the grounds around the Chinn House is taken from a National Park Service archaeological survey of the site and several maps of the area contained in the Manassas National Battlefield Park files. *The Official Military Atlas of the Civil War*, plate III, map 2.
30. *OR*, 12:2:286, 290, 292, 295.
31. Leonard, "Texians at Manassas."
32. *OR*, 12:2:613–14.
33. Warner, *Generals in Gray*, 261–62.
34. *OR*, 12:2:613–14, 618.
35. Ibid., 615–16; "An Illustrated History of the Fourth Texas Infantry," http://www.pha.jhu.edu/~dag/4thtex/history/history.html, accessed March 23, 2011.
36. Robert Campbell Diary, 86, MNBP.
37. Bachman, *Charleston Courier*, September 11, 1862; *OR*, 12:2:607.
38. *OR*, 12:2:600–3.
39. Ibid., 500–603.

Chapter 3. "Perfect Storms of Bullets"

1. Ibid., 609; letter to editor from "Potomac," written September 23, 1862, *Atlanta Southern Confederacy*, October 11, 1862.
2. George B. Fox to father, August 31, 1862, George B. Fox Papers, Cincinnati Historical Society (CHS hereafter); *OR*, 12:2:609–11.
3. Johnston, *Four Years a Soldier*, 178–79.
4. Eppa Hunton's Report on Second Manassas, James L. Kemper Papers, University of Virginia.
5. *OR*, 12:2:286, 293; Hurst, *Journal History*, 40.
6. *OR*, 12:2:286; T. C. H. Smith Papers, OHS, 185–87.

7. In Evans's approach to Chinn Ridge, Col. F. W. McMaster reported two batteries about the Chinn House, "one on each side." Capt. King Bryan of the 5th Texas described the second battery on Chinn Ridge as being "on the left and rear" of McLean's left wing. Bryan also claimed the capture of two caissons from that battery. Cooper's Pennsylvania battery reported losing two caissons on Chinn Ridge and described its position as being near the Chinn House. *OR*, 12:2:619–20, 633; James A. Gardner, Address at the Dedication of the Monument at Gettysburg for the First Pennsylvania Light Artillery, Cooper's Battery B, September 11, 1889; J. S. Fullerton to his wife, August 31, 1862, *Lawrence Journal*, September 6, 1862.

8. Conrad, "From Glory to Contention," *Civil War Times Illustrated*, September 1983, 33–38; Kim Holien File on Nathan G. Evans.

9. Owen, *Campfire Stories and Reminiscences*, 12.

10. Conrad, "From Glory to Contention," 35; *OR*, 12:2:628.

11. *OR*, 12:2:631; M. V. Smith Reminiscences, 17; Lowery, "My Experience . . . in the 17th South Carolina Volunteers," South Caroliniana Library, 16.

12. *OR*, 12:2:609; Barrett, *The Confederacy Is on Her Way up the Spout*, 75; "Ben to Dear Father," September 1, 1862, *Zanesville Daily Courier*, September 5, 1862.

13. "John Marshall Whilden, Boy Major of the Coast Rangers," http://www.awod.com/cwchas/johnw1.html, accessed April 14, 2008; *Charleston Daily Courier*, September 10, 1862.

14. *OR*, 12:2:631, 633, 636.

15. Several Texans reported hearing the command "Forward, Legion!" and seeing the Palmetto State flag. In consequence, they assumed that it was the Hampton Legion of Hood's brigade advancing on their left. It was not. The Hampton Legion had advanced and fought the Ohioans until Evans's brigade came up. The Hampton Legion then retired from the battle when Evans's South Carolinians arrived. *OR*, 12:2:611, 618, 631; Leonard, "Texians at Manassas"; Robert Campbell Diary, MNBP, 86.

16. Reid, *Ohio in the War*, 2:421.

17. "Letter from a Member of Holcombe's Legion," *Charleston Courier*, September 24, 1862.

18. OR, 12:2:737, 750; Report of Fauquier Artillery of the Second Battle of Bull Run, Edward Porter Alexander Papers, University of North Carolina; Hurst, *Journal History*, 41; Erskine Carson, "Narrative of the Experience of Erksine Carson, 73rd Reg't. Ohio Veteran Volunteer Infantry, in the Civil War," MNBP.

19. *OR*, 12:2:618, 631.

20. Ibid.

21. Gates, "John Hugh Means," *South Carolina Biographical Dictionary*, 225.

22. Letter of Ben, 25th Ohio, September 1, 1862, *Zanesville Daily Courier*, September 5, 1862.

23. *OR*, 12:2:636.

24. Hurst, *Journal History*, 40–41; T. C. H. Smith Papers, OHS, 180.

25. There is some controversy over the origination of the orders for McLean to change front. McLean does not mention receiving orders from Schenck, but Lt. William H. Cheesbrough, Schenck's aide-de-camp, reported that

Schenck directed McLean to change front. Additionally, the Ohioans who successfully changed front make numerous references to Schenck being on the scene at that point in the battle. Pope was highly complimentary of Schenck, crediting the "protracted resistance" by McLean's brigade to Schenck's "presence and the fearless exposure of his person during these attacks." *OR*, 12:2:282.

26. Report of Brig. Gen. Zealous B. Tower, T. C. H. Smith Papers, OHS; Hanna, "From Manassas to Antietam."
27. *OR*, 12:2:341.
28. Warner, *Generals in Blue*, 510; Vautier, *History of the 88th Pennsylvania Volunteers*, 58; Charles S. McClenthen to father, September 4, 1862, Charles S. McClenthen Letters, Cornell University; Tower's Report, T. C. H. Smith Papers, OHS.
29. Tower's Report, T. C. H. Smith Papers, OHS; John D. Vautier Papers, Diary, USAMHI.
30. John D. Vautier Papers, Diary, USAMHI.
31. *OR*, 12:2:389–92; Report of Major Davis Tillson, Chief of Artillery, Third Corps, Army of Virginia, Lewis Leigh Papers, USAMHI.
32. Vautier, *History of the 88th Pennsylvania Volunteers*, 54.
33. *OR*, 12:2:389–90; McClenthen to father, September 4, 1862, Charles McClenthen Letters, Cornell University; Leonard, "Texians at Manassas."
34. H. T. Owen, "Reminiscences of the War," Library of Virginia.
35. Ibid.
36. *OR*, 12:2:389.

Chapter 4. "We Went for Them"

1. William W. Potter, "The 55th Ohio Regiment at Groveton," *Norwalk Experiment*, October 27, 1862; Jesse Bowsher and A. S. Wormley to D. Bowsher, September 15, 1862, *Wyandot Pioneer*, September 26, 1862.
2. *OR*, 12:2:287, 291, 633, 636; Jesse Bowsher and A. S. Wormley to D. Bowsher, September 15, 1862, *Wyandot Pioneer*, September 26, 1862; A. S. Wormley to L. A. Brunner, October 7, 1862, *Wyandot Pioneer*, October 17, 1862. Nathaniel McLean to John R. Ropes, October 6, 1897, John C. Ropes Papers, Boston University.
3. *OR*, 12:2:618, 620; Leonard, "Texians at Manassas"; Robert Campbell Diary, MNBP, 87.
4. McLean claimed that he rallied the 25th and 73rd Ohio and brought them back into line of battle after the 55th Ohio changed front, but it is clear from the official reports from those two units that they did not rally as a unit on Chinn Ridge. McLean only managed to reform a small number of men from these two units. The rest retreated toward Chinn Branch and the woods beyond. *OR* 12:2:287, 290, 293.
5. *OR*, 11:1:578.
6. Hunter, *Four Years in the Ranks*, Virginia Historical Society.
7. Warner, *Generals in Gray*, 63; *OR*, 12:2:626, 51:1:136.
8. Dooley, *John Dooley Confederate Soldier*, 21.
9. Hunter, *Johnny Reb and Billy Yank*, 248–49.

10. Johnston, *Four Years a Soldier*, 180–81; Mesnard Memoirs, Firelands Historical Society, 13; *OR*, 12:2:291.
11. *OR*, 12:2:626, 51:1:136.
12. Sgt. J. K. Simmons of the 28th Virginia wrote that "Hunton was following the retreating line of skirmishers" that had fallen back on the south side of the house at Kemper's first appearance at this point in the battle. Simmons, *A Touch of History*, 33.
13. Ibid.
14. Hagood, "Memoirs," South Caroliniana Library; Vautier, *History of the 88th Pennsylvania Volunteers*, 55–56.
15. Report of Hartsuff's brigade, September 8, 1862, MNBP; William R. Rankin Notebook, Brocky Nicely manuscript.
16. Letter of E. N. Whittier, September 5, 1862, *Portland Daily Advertiser*, September 10, 1862.
17. Joseph A. McLean to wife, August 22, 1862, MNBP.
18. W. J. Rannells to Mrs. Col. J. A. McLean, October 3, 1862, MNBP.
19. Letter of Capt. W. K. Bachman, *Charleston Courier*, September 17, 1862.
20. W. B. Judkins, "History of Co. G, 22nd Ga Regiment," Sarah Hightower Regional Library, Rome, GA.
21. Houghton, *Two Boys in the Civil War and After*, 124.
22. *OR*, 12:2:282, 287; Robert C. Schenck conversation with T. C. H. Smith, August 30, 1864, T. C. H. Smith Papers, OHS; Edward H. Allen to T. C. H. Smith, October 16, 1868, T. C. H. Smith Papers, OHS; Nathaniel C. McLean to John C. Ropes, October 6, 1897, John C. Ropes Papers, Boston University.
23. Woodhead, *Voices of the Civil War*, 144.
24. Nathaniel C. McLean to John Ropes, John C. Ropes Papers, Boston University; H. E. Rosenberger, "Ohiowa Soldier," 118; "From the 55th Ohio," *Wyandot Pioneer*, September 26, 1862.
25. Reid, *Ohio in the War*, 2:730–31.
26. Griffin stated that Webster was commanding an Ohio regiment but was mistaken in that regard. Webster's regiment had reinforced the 55th Ohio shortly before Fletcher went down. William H. Griffin Papers, Mississippi Department of Archives and History.
27. Letter of Sergeant C. D. Hardy, 12th Massachusetts, *Rochester Democrat and American*, September 24, 1862.
28. Faulk, "The Part Taken by the 11th Pa. on the Plains of Manassas," *National Tribune*, February 19, 1891.
29. Wood, *Reminiscences of Big I*, 32; Johnston, *Four Years a Soldier*, 181; *OR*, 12:3:625–27; Hunter, *Johnny Reb*, 248–49.
30. Dooley, *John Dooley Confederate Soldier*, 21–22.
31. Mesnard Memoirs, Firelands Historical Society; Jesse Bowsher and Augustus S. Wormley to D. Bowsher, September 12, 1862, *Wyandot Pioneer*, September 26, 1862.
32. Nathaniel C. McLean to John Ropes, John C. Ropes Papers, Boston University; *National Tribune*, March 15, 1917.
33. Mesnard Memoirs, Firelands Historical Society, 14.
34. Vautier, *History of the 88th Pennsylvania Volunteers*, 56.

Chapter 5. "We Can Keep Them Back"
1. *OR*, 12:2:284–85.
2. *OR*, 12:2:283.
3. *OR*, 12:2:301; Schurz, 218.
4. *OR*, 12:2:307–8; Hagood, "Memoirs," South Caroliniana Library.
5. Hunter, *Johnny Reb*, 250.
6. *OR*, 12:2:307; Report of Lt. Col. Ernest Von Holmsted, 41st NY, September 14, 1862; Affidavit of E. B. Coleman, 18th Virginia, H. T. Owen Papers, Library of Virginia.
7. *OR*, 12:2:307–8, 571, 575, 51:1:135; Hunter, *Johnny Reb*, 249.
8. *OR*, 12:2:307–8, 571, 575.
9. *OR*, 12:2:301, 312, 314–15; Nachtingel, *History of the 75th Regiment, Pa Vols.*, 18; Louis Biskey Diary, 45th New York Infantry, FSNMP.
10. *OR*, 12:2:579; Charles W. Williams, aide-de-camp to Gen. D. R. Jones, Testimony, Case of Fitz John Porter, 257.
11. Ibid., 12:2:583, 592.
12. Ibid.
13. Ibid., 301, 312, 314–15; Nachtingel, *History of the 75th Regiment, Pa Vols.*, 18.
14. *OR*, 12:2:301, 593.
15. Hunter, *Johnny Reb*, 252.
16. Report of Colonel George Von Amsberg, 45th New York, MNBP.
17. Louis Biskey Diary, FSNMP.
18. Hennessy, *Map Study*, 379.
19. *OR*, 12:2:305–6.
20. Schurz, *The Autobiography of Carl Shurz*, 196.
21. George C. Parker Letters, October 15–18, 1862, MNBP.
22. Powell, *The Fifth Army Corps*, 539.
23. Ames, "The Second Bull Run," 402.
24. Ibid.
25. "Letter from a Wheeling Boy in the Second Virginia Regiment," *Wheeling Daily Intelligencer*, September 22, 1862.
26. William R. Rankin Notebook, Brocky A. Nicely Files, Staunton, Virginia.
27. Paulus, *Papers of General Robert Huston Milroy*, 92.
28. William R. Rankin Notebook, Brocky A. Nicely Files, Staunton, Virginia.
29. Robert H. Milroy to his wife, September 4, 1862, contained in Paulus, *Papers of General Robert Huston Milroy*, 92; F. S. Jacobs, "The 82nd in Battle," *Hardin County Republican*, October 10, 1862.
30. Choice, "Memoirs of My Four Years."
31. *OR*, 12:2:579.
32. "Letter from Capt. J. B. Moor of the 'Columbus Volunteers,' 17th Ga. Regiment," *Daily Sun* (Columbus, Georgia), September 8, 1862.
33. Robert Campbell Journal, MNBP, 88–89.
34. J. J. Mastern Letter, *The Warren (PA) Mail*, September 30, 1862; *OR*, 12:2:583–85.
35. Woodford, *History of the Third Pennsylvania Reserve*, 162.
36. "From the Pennsylvania Reserves," *Lancaster Daily Evening Express*, September 10, 1862.
37. M. O. Young Recollections, Atlanta Historical Center.

38. Dougherty, "An Eyewitness Account of Second Bull Run," 1:8:42–43.
39. Robert H. Milroy to his wife, September 4, 1862, in Paulus, *Papers of General Robert Huston Milroy*, 91–92.
40. Ibid.; Reese, *Sykes Regular Infantry Division*, 122.
41. *OR*, 12:2:321–22; F. S. Jacobs, "The 82nd in Battle," *Hardin County Republican*, October 10, 1862.
42. "From the 86th Regiment N.Y.S.V.," *Addison Advertiser*, September 10, 1862.
43. "Letter from Capt. Shoemaker," *Elmira Weekly Journal*, September 6, 1862.
44. Milroy to his wife, September 4, 1862, in Paulus, *Papers of General Robert Huston Milroy*, 91–92.
45. *OR*, 12:2:579; Letter from the Phillips Legion, *The Southern Watchman* (Athens, Georgia), October 1, 1862.
46. Gallagher, *Fighting for the Confederacy*, 249.
47. "Letter of General A. R. Wright," *Augusta Daily Constitutionalist*, September 17, 1862; "From the 48th Georgia Regiment," *Augusta Daily Constitutionalist*, September 20, 1862.
48. *OR*, 12:2:497.
49. Milroy to his wife, September 4, 1862, in Paulus, *Papers of General Robert Huston Milroy*, 91–92.
50. Ibid.
51. *OR*, 12:2:363–64.
52. Reese, *Sykes' Regular Infantry Division*, 43, 60; George W. Cullum, *Biographical Register of the Officers and Graduates of the U. S. Military Academy at West Point, N.Y.*, vol. 1, 321.
53. Ames, "The Second Bull Run," 402.
54. Private Henry Brown to his parents, September 6, 1862, http://www.esp designs.com/letters/1862/Letter18_9_06_62.htm, accessed August 3, 2010; Walcott, *Twenty-First Massachusetts*, 104–5; *OR*, 11:2:420.
55. Walcott, 104.
56. Ibid.
57. Ibid.
58. "Letter of General A. R. Wright," *Augusta Daily Constitutionalist*, September 17, 1862; *OR*, 12:2:323, 483; "Letter from a Wheeling Boy," *Wheeling Daily Intelligencer*, September 22, 1862.
59. Ephraim Bisel to his brother, September 10, 1862, in *The Clinton Democrat* (Lock Haven, PA), September 25, 1862.

Chapter 6. "We Are Friends Now"
1. George C. Parker Letters, October 15–18, 1862, MNBP.
2. Hennessy, *Map Study*, 463, 472; McPherson, *The Atlas of the Civil War*, 76.
3. Johnston, *Four Years a Soldier*, 182.
4. Hagood, "Memoirs," 72, South Caroliniana Library.
5. Carson, "Narrative of the Experience of Erskine Carson, 73rd Reg't. Ohio Veteran Volunteer Infantry, in the Civil War," MNBP.
6. Ibid.
7. Houghton, *Two Boys in the Civil War*, 126–27.
8. Samuel C. Lowry Papers, South Caroliniana Library.

9. Letter of Captain C. R. Jennings, *Rochester Union and American,* September 9, 1862.

10. Theodore Fogle Papers, Emory University.

11. Polley, *A Soldier's Letters,* 78.

12. "William Mahone, 1826–1895," http://www.encyclopediavirginia.org/Mahone_William_1826–1895, accessed August 14, 2010.

13. "Col. Brodhead's Letter," undated newspaper clipping in author's collection; Jesse Bowsher and A. S. Wormley to D. Bowsher, September 15, 1862, *Wyandot Pioneer,* September 26, 1862.

14. Nathaniel McLean to John C. Ropes, October 6, 1897, John C. Ropes Papers, Boston University; Ephraim Bisel to Dear Brother, September 10, 1862, in *The Clinton Democrat* (Lock Haven, PA), September 25, 1862.

15. Address of General Pope, *New York Tribune,* September 18, 1862.

16. Williams, *From the Cannon's Mouth.*

17. N.G.S., Letter from the 25th Ohio Regiment, Alexandria, September 6, 1862, *The Freemont Journal,* September 19, 1862.

Chapter 7. Union Disaster Averted

1. At Chancellorsville, Luvas and Nelson place Lee's engaged strength at 48,080 and his losses at 12,299 for a loss rate of 25.6 percent. On the Union side of the ledger, the Army of the Potomac lost 15,818 out of 104,891 engaged for a 15 percent casualty rate. At Second Manassas, Hennessy places Lee's strength at 55,000 and his losses at roughly 8,700 for a loss rate of 15.8 percent. Pope is generally attributed to having 75,000 men in his army, but this does not take into account that Maj. Gen. Nathaniel Banks's corps was not present. Pope's effective strength on the battlefield was closer to 65,000 as a result. Losses of nearly 14,000 men during the campaign put his casualty rate at 21.5 percent. William W. Hassler, *One of Lee's Best Men,* 173; Hennessy, *Return to Bull Run,* 441, 456; Hennessy, *Map Study,* 463; Luvas and Nelson, *The U.S. Army War College Guide to the Battles of Chancellorsville and Fredericksburg,* 349.

2. *OR,* 12:2:564–66; Sorrel, *Recollections of a Confederate Staff Officer,* 99; Everett, *Chaplain Davis and Hood's Texas Brigade,* 118.

3. Report of Captain Robert M. Stribling, Fauquier Artillery, Edward Porter Alexander Papers, University of North Carolina.

4. *OR,* 12:2:563.

5. Nathaniel McLean to John C. Ropes, October 6, 1897, John C. Ropes Papers, Boston University.

6. Pope, "The Second Battle of Bull Run," in Buel and Johnston, *Battles and Leaders of the Civil War,* 487.

7. Fletcher, *Rebel Private,* 54.

Bibliography

Manuscripts
Alabama Department of Archives and History
    John Reed Journal
Atlanta Historical Center
    Matthew Nunnally Letters
    M. O. Young Recollections
Bucknell University
    George Shorkley Diary
Cincinnati Historical Society
    George B. Fox Letters
Cornell University
    Charles S. McClenthen Letters
Duke University
    W. S. Shockey Papers
Emory University
    Theodore Fogle Papers
Firelands Historical Society, Norwalk, Ohio
    Captain Charles B. Gambee Diary
    Sergeant Luther B. Mesnard Memoirs
Fredericksburg and Spotsylvania National Military Park
    Louis Biskey Diary
    M. V. Smith Reminiscences
Georgia Department of Archives and History
    W. B. Jennings Memoirs
    M. O. Young, "History of the First Brigade"
Hightower Regional Library, Rome, Georgia
    W. B. Judkins, "History of Co. G, 22nd Georgia Regiment"

Hill Junior College History Complex
    Nicholas Pomeroy Letters
    H. G. Simpson
Library of Congress
    Samuel P. Heintzelman Journal
    Marsena Patrick Diary
    Fitz John Porter Papers
Library of Virginia
    E. B. Coleman Affidavit
    H. T. Owen Papers
    John F. Sale Papers
Manassas Museum
    Hutchinson Family Newspaper Clippings
Manassas National Battlefield Park
    Erskine Carson to Colonel Orland Smith, January 6, 1869
    Narrative of the Experience of Erskine Carson, 73rd Reg't., Ohio Veteran
        Volunteer Infantry
    William Choice, "Memoirs of My Four Years in the War Between the States"
    "94th Regiment New York Vols. In Pope's Virginia Campaign, 1862"
    Joseph A. McLean Letters
    George C. Parker Letters
    W. J. Rannells to Mrs. Col. J. A. McLean, Oct. 3, 1862
    Report of 2nd New York Light Artillery
    Report of 8th New York Infantry
    Report of 29th New York Infantry
    Report of 41st New York Infantry
    Report of 45th New York Infantry
    Report of 83rd New York Infantry
    Abraham Rudisill, "Battle of Second Bull Run"
    Major Allan Rutherford Memorandum Book, 83rd New York
    "Statement of Experience in action of 83rd Regiment N. Y. S. Vol's"
    Robert Campbell Diary
Massachusetts Historical Society
    Fiske Family Papers
Mississippi Department of Archives and History
    William H. Griffin Papers
Military Historical Society of Massachusetts, Boston University
    John C. Ropes Papers
National Archives
    Record of Events, 25th Ohio Infantry
New York Historical Society
    Alfred Davenport Papers
North Carolina Historical Commission
    The Shotwell Papers
Ohio Historical Society
    T. C. H. Smith Papers

Pennsylvania History and Museum Commission
    John Taggart Memoirs
Private Collections
    Kim Holien, Nathan B. Evans File
    Brocky A. Nicely, "The Regimental History of the Palmetto Sharpshooter
        Regiment"
Sarah Hightower Regional Library, Rome, Georgia
    W. B. Judkins, "History of Co. G, 22nd Ga Regiment"
South Caroliniana Library, University of South Carolina
    James R. Hagood, "Memoirs of the First South Carolina Regiment of Volun-
        teer Infantry"
    Samuel C. Lowry Papers
    Joseph J. Murray Letters
Southern Historical Collection, University of North Carolina
    Edward Porter Alexander Papers
United States Army Military History Institute
    Civil War Times Illustrated Collection
        Frank P. Jennings Reminiscences, January 7, 1867
    Lewis Leigh Collection
        Report of Major Davis Tillson, Chief of Artillery, Third Corps
            Army of Virginia, September 30, 1862
    John D. Vautier Papers
    Abraham Rudisill Papers
University of Virginia
    Report of Colonel Eppa Hunton in James L. Kemper Papers
Virginia Historical Society
    Benjamin L. Farinholt Diary
    Alexander Hunter, "Four Years in the Ranks"
Western Historical Manuscript Collection, University of Missouri
    Alfred Avery Lamkin Diary

Newspapers
Addison (NY) Advertiser
Atlanta Southern Confederacy
Augusta Daily Constitutionalist
Bangor (ME) Daily Whig and Courier
Belmont (OH) Chronicle
Berks and Schuylkill Journal (PA)
Bucyrus (OH) Weekly Journal
Camden (SC) Confederate
Carolina Spartan (Spartanburg, SC)
Charleston (SC) Daily Courier
Clearfield (PA) Republican
Cleveland Plain Dealer
Clinton (PA) Democrat
Columbus (GA) Daily Sun

Corning (NY) Weekly Journal
Cumberland Valley (PA) Spirit
Daily Lynchburg Virginian
Elmira (NY) Weekly Journal
Freemont (OH) Journal
Hardin County (OH) Republican
Houston Tri-Weekly Telegraph
Ironton (OH) Register
Lancaster (PA) Daily Express
Lawrence (PA) Journal
Lebanon (PA) Courier
Macon (GA) Telegraph
Manassas Journal
National Tribune (Washington, D.C.) (*NT* hereafter)
New York Tribune
Norwalk (OH) Experiment
Norwalk (OH) Reflector
Painesville (OH) Telegraph
Philadelphia Daily Evening Bulletin
Philadelphia Weekly Times
Portland (ME) Daily Advertiser
Quincy (MA) Patriot Ledger
Rochester (NY) Democrat and American
Rome (GA) Tri-Weekly Courier
Seneca (OH) Advertiser
Springfield (MA) Daily Republican
Tiffin (OH) Tribune
Weekly Banner (Athens, Georgia)
Wheeling (WV) Daily Intelligencer
Wyandot (OH) Pioneer
Xenia (OH) Torchlight
Zanesville (OH) Daily Courier

Articles

Ames, John W. "The Second Bull Run." *Overland Monthly* 8 (1872): 400–5.

Berkeley, Norborne. "Eighth Virginia's Part in Second Manassas." *Southern Historical Society Papers* 37 (1909): 313–16.

Conrad, James L. "From Glory to Contention: The Sad History of 'Shanks' Evans." *Civil War Times Illustrated* (September 1983).

Dougherty, William E. "An Eyewitness Account of Second Bull Run." *American History Illustrated* 1, no. 8 (December 1966): 30–43.

Faulk, Phil K. "The Part Taken by the 11th Pa. on the Plains of Manassas." *NT*, February 19, 1891.

Gardner, James A. "Address at the Dedication of the Monument at Gettysburg for the First Pennsylvania Light Artillery." *The (Shippensburg) Chronicle*, August 25, 1921.

Gates, Robert W. "John Hugh Means." Winnsboro, NC, privately published, 1983.

Goodrich, Ira B. "Second Bull Run." *NT*, May 4, 1893.

Hanna, Thomas L. "From Manassas to Antietam." *NT*, March 2 and 9, 1905.

Longstreet, James, "Our March Against Pope." *Century Illustrated Monthly Magazine* 31, no. 4 (February 1886).

Monroe, J. Albert. "Reminiscences of the War of the Rebellion of 1861–65." *Personal Narratives of the Battles of the Rebellion, Being Papers Read Before the Rhode Island Soldiers and Sailors Historical Society*. Providence, RI: N. Bangs Williams, 1881.

———. "Battery D, First Rhode Island Light Artillery, at the Second Battle of Bull Run." *Personal Narratives of the Battles of the Rebellion, Being Papers Read Before the Rhode Island Soldiers and Sailors Historical Society*. Providence, RI: published by the society, 1890.

Moor, Capt. J. B., of the Columbus Volunteers. "17th Ga. Regiment." *Daily Sun* (Columbus, Georgia), September 8, 1862.

Rathbun, Isaac R. "A Civil War Diary: The Diary of Isaac R. Rathbun, Company D, 86th N.Y. Volunteers, August 23, 1862–January 20, 1863." *New York History* 36 (1955): 336–45.

Rosenberger, H. E., ed. "Ohiowa Soldier." *Annals of Iowa* (Fall 1961): 11–148.

Shearer, Robert A. "McDowell at Bull Run." *NT*, June 23, 1908.

Spooner, B. "Second Bull Run." *NT*, July 28, 1892.

Sumner, George C. "Recollections of Service in Battery D, First Rhode Island Light Artillery." *Personal Narratives of the Battles of the Rebellion, Being Papers Read Before the Rhode Island Soldiers and Sailors Historical Society*. Providence, RI: N. Bangs Williams, 1891.

Vautier, John. "Ricketts' Division in Pope's Campaign." *Grand Army Scout and Soldiers Mail*, December 22, 1883.

Watson, J. M. "As to Saving Washington." *NT*, March 11, 1897.

Webster, S. D. "General Irvin McDowell." *NT*, May 5, 1892.

Wise, G. W. "A Serviceable Prisoner." *CV* 29 (1929): 236.

Official Documents

United States Congress. Senate Executive Document 37; *Proceedings and Report of the Board of Army Officers in the Case of Fitz John Porter*. 4 Parts. Washington: 1879.

United States War Department. *The Official Military Atlas of the Civil War*. Washington: Government Printing Office, 1891–1895.

United States War Department. *The War of the Rebellion: A Compilation of the Official Records of the Union and Confederate Armies*. 128 vols. Washington: 1881–1902.

Books

Alden, Luther E. *Secretary's Annual Circular-Twelfth Massachusetts (Webster) Regiment Association*. Boston: Twelfth (Webster) Regiment Association, 1908.

Andrews, W. H. *Footprints of a Regiment: A Recollection of the 1st Georgia Regulars, 1861–1865*. Atlanta, GA: Longstreet Press, 1992.

Andrews, W. J. *Sketch of Company K., 23rd South Carolina Volunteers in the Civil War, from 1862–1865*. Richmond, n.d.

Bacon, William J. *Memorial of William Kirkland Bacon, Late Adjutant of the Twenty-Sixth Regiment of New York State Volunteers.* Utica, NY: Roberts, Printer, 1863.

Baldwin, James J. III. *The Struck Eagle: A Biography of Brigadier General Micah Jenkins, and a History of the Fifth South Carolina Volunteers and the Palmetto Sharpshooters.* Shippensburg, PA: Burd Street Press, 1996.

Bates, Samuel P. *History of Pennsylvania Volunteers, 1861–5.* Harrisburg: B. Singerly, State Printer, 1869–71.

Brown, Philip F. *Reminiscences of the War: Company "C" 12th Virginia Infantry Mahone's Brigade.* Richmond: Whittet & Shepperson, Printers, 1917.

Buel, Clarence Clough, and Robert Underwood Johnston, eds. *Battles and Leaders of the Civil War.* 4 vols. New York: The Century Co., 1884–1887.

Butts, Joseph Tyler, ed. *A Gallant Captain of the Civil War, Being the Record of the Extraordinary Adventures of Frederick Otto Baron Von Fritsch.* New York: F. T. Neely, 1902.

Coker, James L. *History of Company G. 9th South Carolina Regiment, Infantry, and Company E. 6th South Carolina Regiment, Infantry, South Carolina Army.* (n.p.: 1899).

Cook, Benjamin F. *History of the Twelfth Massachusetts.* Boston: Twelfth (Webster) Regiment Association, 1882.

Cullum, George W. *Biographical Register of the Officers and Graduates of the U. S. Military Academy at West Point, N.Y. from Its Establishment.* New York: D. Van Nostrand, 1868.

Culp, Edward C. *The 25th Ohio Vet. Vol. Infantry in the War for the Union.* Topeka: G. W. Crane and Co. Printers, 1885.

Current, Richard, N. *Encyclopedia of the Confederacy.* New York: Macmillan, 1993.

Davis, Charles E. Jr. *Three Years in the Army: The Story of the Thirteenth Massachusetts Volunteers from July 16, 1861, to August 1, 1864.* Boston: Estes and Lauriat, 1894.

Davis, Nicholas A. *The Campaign from Texas to Maryland.* Richmond: Presbyterian Committee of Publication of the Confederate States, 1863.

Dawes, Rufus R. *Service with the Sixth Wisconsin Infantry.* Marietta, OH: E. R. Alderman, 1890.

Dooley, John. *John Dooley Confederate Soldier; His War Journal.* South Bend, IN: University of Notre Dame Press, 1963.

Dowdey, Clifford. *Lee's Wartime Papers.* Boston: Little, Brown, 1961.

Edwards, Captain W. H. *A Condensed History of the 17th Regiment S.C.V., C.S.A.* Columbia, SC: Press of the R. L. Bryan Co., 1908.

Everett, Donald E., ed. *Chaplain Davis and Hood's Texas Brigade.* San Antonio, TX: Principia Press of Trinity University, 1962.

Fletcher, William A. *Rebel Private: Front and Rear: Memoirs of a Confederate Soldier.* New York: Dutton, 1995.

Fowler, Andrew L. *Memoirs of the Late Adjt. Andrew L. Fowler of the 51st N.Y.V. Who Fell at the Battle of Antietam Bridge, September 17th, 1862.* "Compiled by a Friend." New York: Ferris & Pratt, Printers, 1863.

Gallagher, Gary W., ed. *Fighting for the Confederacy: The Personal Recollections of General Edward Alexander Porter.* Chapel Hill: University of North Carolina Press, 1989.

Gatell, Frank Otto. "John McLean." In *The Justices of the United States Supreme Court, 1789–1969: Their Lives and Major Opinions,* edited by Leon Friedman and Fred L. Israel. 5 vols. New York: Chelsea House Publishers, 1969.

Gold, Thomas D. *History of Clarke County, Virginia, and Its Connection with the War Between States.* Berryville, VA: 1914.

Hardin, Martin D., *History of the Twelfth Regiment Pennsylvania Reserve Corps.* New York: printed by author, 1890.

Hassler, William W., ed. *One of Lee's Best Men: The Civil War Letters of General William Dorsey Pender.* Chapel Hill: University of North Carolina Press, 1999.

Heller, J. Roderick III, and Carolynn Ayres Heller, eds. *The Confederacy Is on Her Way up the Spout: Letters to South Carolina, 1861–1864.* Athens: University of Georgia Press, 1992.

Hennessy, John J. *Return to Bull Run: The Campaign and Battle of Second Manassas.* New York: Simon & Schuster, 1993.

———. *Second Manassas Battlefield Map Study.* Lynchburg, VA: H. E. Howard, Co. 1991.

Hill, Archibald F. *Our Boys.* Philadelphia: John E. Potter, 1864.

Hood, J. B. *Advance and Retreat: Personal Experiences in the United States and Confederate State Armies.* (New Orleans, 1880).

Houghton, W. R., and M. B. Houghton. *Two Boys in the Civil War and After.* Montgomery: Paragon Press, 1912.

Hoyt, James A. *The Palmetto Riflemen.* Greenville, SC: Hoyt and Keys, Printers, 1885.

Hunter, Alexander. *Johnny Reb and Billy Yank.* New York: Neale Publishing Company, 1905.

Hunton, Eppa. *Autobiography of Eppa Hunton.* Richmond, VA: William Byrd Press, 1933.

Hurst, Samuel H. *Journal History of the Seventy-Third Ohio Volunteer Infantry.* Chillicothe: S. H. Hurst, 1866.

Hussey, George W. *History of the Ninth Regiment New York State Militia.* New York: Press of J. S. Ogilvie, 1889.

Irby, Richard. *Historical Sketch of the Nottoway Grays.* Richmond, VA: J. W. Ferguson & Son, 1878.

Johnston, David E. *Four Years a Soldier.* Princeton, WV: 1887.

Ladley, Oscar Derostus. *Hearth and Knapsack: The Ladley Letters, 1857–1880.* Edited by Carl M. Becker and Ritchie Thomas. Athens: Ohio University Press, 1988.

Lang, Theodore F. *Loyal West Virginia from 1861 to 1865.* Baltimore: Deutsch Publishing, 1895.

Locke, William Henry. *The Story of the Regiment.* Philadelphia: J. B. Lippincott, 1868.

Longstreet, James. *From Manassas to Appomattox.* Dallas: Dallas Publishing, 1896.

Luvaas, Jay, and Harold W. Nelson, eds. *The U.S. Army War College Guide to the Battles of Chancellorsville & Fredericksburg.* Carlisle, PA: South Mountain Press, 1988.

McPherson, James M, ed. *The Atlas of the Civil War.* Philadelphia: Running Press, 2005.

Meyers, Augustus. *Ten Years in the Ranks of the U.S. Army.* New York: Stirling Press, 1914.

Nachtigall, Herrmann. *History of the 75th Pennsylvania Infantry.* New York: Druck von C. B. Kretschman, 1886.

Osborn, Captain Hartwell. *Trials and Triumphs, The Record of the Fifty-Fifth Ohio Volunteer Infantry.* Chicago: A. C. McClurg, 1904.

Owen, Dock. *Campfire Stories and Reminiscences.* Greenwood, SC (n.p., n.d.).

Parker, Thomas H. *History of the 51st Regiment of P.V. and V.V.* Philadelphia: King and Baird, 1869.

Paulus, Margaret B., ed. *Papers of General Robert Huston Milroy.* 2 vols. (n.p., 1965).

Polley, Joseph Benjamin. *Hood's Texas Brigade: Its Marches, Its Battles, Its Achievements.* New York: Neale Publishing, 1910.

———. *A Soldier's Letters to Charming Nellie.* New York: Neale Publishing, 1908.

Powell, William H. *The Fifth Army Corps: A Record of Operations During the Civil War of the United States of America, 1861–1865.* New York: G. P. Putnam, 1896.

Reese, Timothy J. *Sykes' Regular Infantry Division, 1861–1864: A History of Regular United States Infantry Operations in the Civil War's Eastern Theater.* Jefferson, NC: McFarland, 1990.

Reid, Whitelaw. *Ohio in the War: Her Statesmen, Generals and Soldiers.* Cincinnati, OH: Moore, Listach and Baldwin, 1868.

Schurz, Carl. *The Autobiography of Carl Schurz.* New York: Scribner, 1961.

Sears, Stephen W. *To the Gates of Richmond: The Peninsula Campaign.* New York: Ticknor & Fields, 1992.

Sherman, William T., *Memoirs of General W. T. Sherman.* New York: Literary Classics of the United States, 1990.

Simmons, J. K. *A Touch of History: The Blue Ridge Rifles, Company A, 28th Virginia Volunteer Infantry, A Roll of Honor and Reminiscences.* Fincastle, VA: Botetourt County Historical Society, 1995.

Smith, Gerald J. *"One of the Most Daring of Men": The Life of Confederate General William Tatum Wofford.* Murfreesboro, TN: Southern Heritage Press, 1997.

Sorrel, Moxley. *Recollections of a Confederate Staff Officer.* New York: Neale Publishing, 1905.

South Carolina Biographical Dictionary. New York: Somerset Publishers, 1994.

Stone, James Madison. *Personal Recollections of the Civil War.* Boston: printed by author, 1918.

Swisher, James K. *Prince of Edisto: Brigadier General Micah Jenkins.* Berryville, VA: Rockbridge Publishing, 1996.

Vautier, John D. *History of the 88th Pennsylvania Volunteers in the War for the Union 1861–1865.* Philadelphia: J. B. Lippincott, 1894.

Warner, Ezra J. *Generals in Blue: Lives of the Union Commanders.* Baton Rouge: Louisiana State University Press, 1964.

———. *Generals in Gray: Lives of the Confederate Commanders.* Baton Rouge: Louisiana State University Press, 1959.

Wehrum, Charles C. *Twelfth Massachusetts (Webster) Regiment Association, Secretary's Annual Circular.* Vol. 9. December 1904.

Whitehorne, Joseph W. A. *The Battle of Second Manassas: Self-Guided Tour.* Washington, DC: Center of Military History, United States Army, 1990.

Williams, Alpheus S. *From the Cannon's Mouth: The Civil War Letters of General Alpheus S. Williams.* Detroit: Wayne State University Press and the Detroit Historical Society, 1959.

Wise, George. *History of the Seventeenth Virginia Infantry, C. S. A.* Baltimore: Kelly, Piet, 1870.

Woodhead, Henry. *Voices of the Civil War: Second Manassas.* New York: Time-Life Books, 1995.

Woodward, E. M. *History of the Third Pennsylvania Reserve.* Trenton, NJ: MacCrellish & Quigley, Printers, 1883.

———. *Our Campaigns or The Marches, Bivouacs, Battles, Incidents of Camp Life and History of Our Regiment During Its Three Years of Service.* Philadelphia: J. E. Potter, 1865.

Wood, William Nathaniel. *Reminiscences of Big I.* Edited by Bell Irvin Wiley. Jackson, TN: McCowat-Mercer Press, 1956.

Worsham, John H. *One of Jackson's Foot Cavalry.* Wilmington, NC: Broadfoot Publishing, 1987. First published 1964 by McCowat-Mercer Press.

Zettler, B. M. *War Stories and School Day Incidents for the Children.* New York: 1912.

Index

About the Author

A LIFELONG STUDENT OF MILITARY HISTORY, Scott C. Patchan has been study-ing the American Civil War in depth for more than twenty-five years. A grad-uate of James Madison University in the Shenandoah Valley of Virginia, he is the author of *The Forgotten Fury: The Battle of Piedmont* (1996) and *Shenandoah Summer: The 1864 Valley Campaign* (2007). He also served as a historical con-sultant and writer for Time-Life Voices of the Civil War's *Shenandoah, 1864* (1998) and has written numerous articles for publications such as *Blue & Gray, North & South,* and *Civil War Magazine.* He is a much sought tour guide, having led scores of tours on the Civil War, the Revolutionary War, Colonial America, and the French and Indian War for the last fifteen years. Patchan serves as a director on the board of the Kernstown Battlefield Association in Winchester, Virginia, and is a member of the Shenandoah Valley Battlefield Foundation's Resource Protection Committee. He has twice served as presi-dent of Bull Run Civil War Round Table in Manassas and Centreville, Vir-ginia, and is active in battlefield preservation on many fronts. He currently resides with his wife and children in Prince William County, Virginia, within a few miles of the Manassas Battlefield.